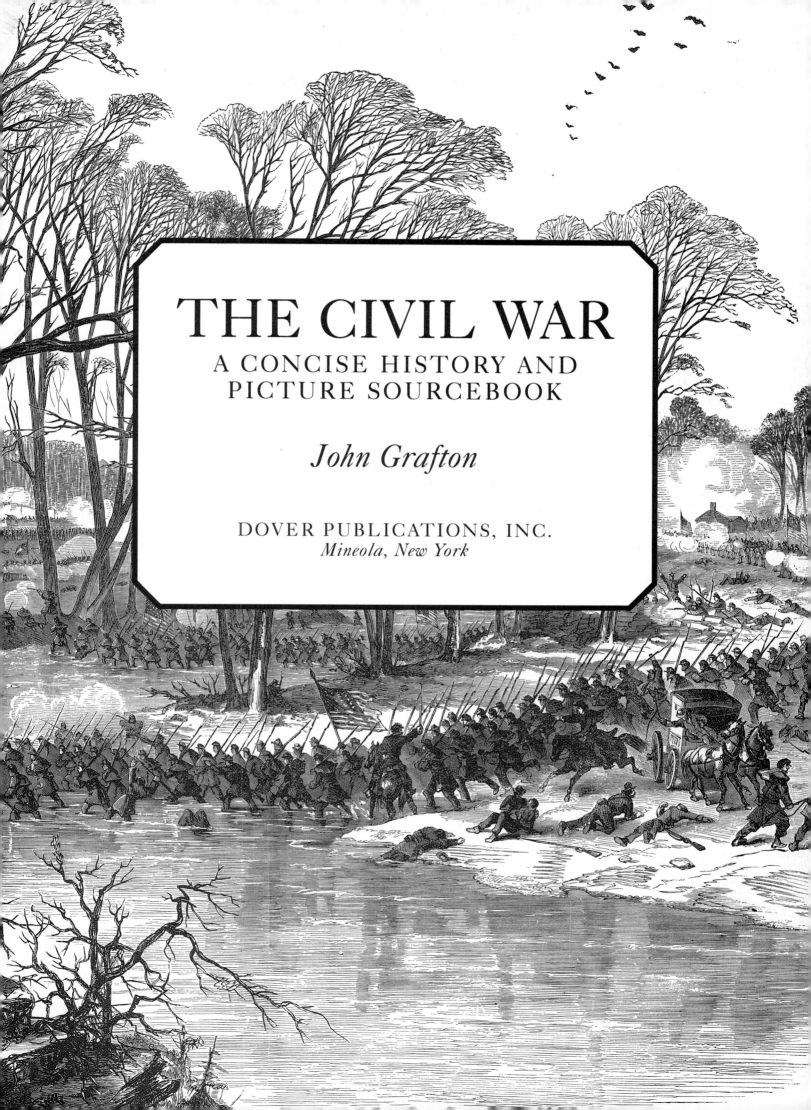

# THE CIVIL WAR
## A CONCISE HISTORY AND PICTURE SOURCEBOOK

*John Grafton*

DOVER PUBLICATIONS, INC.
*Mineola, New York*

*Title page:* The Union Army of the Cumberland on the advance at Stones River, Tennessee, January 2, 1863.

*Bibliographical Note*

*The Civil War: A Concise History and Picture Sourcebook* is a new work, first published by Dover Publications, Inc., in 2003.

DOVER *Pictorial Archive* SERIES

This book belongs to the Dover Pictorial Archive Series. You may use the designs and illustrations for graphics and crafts applications, free and without special permission, provided that you include no more than ten in the same publication or project. (For permission for additional use, please write to Permissions Department, Dover Publications, Inc., 31 East 2nd Street, Mineola, N.Y. 11501.)

However, republication or reproduction of any illustration by any other graphic service, whether it be in a book or in any other design resource, is strictly prohibited.

*Library of Congress Cataloging-in-Publication Data*

The Civil War: a concise history and picture sourcebook / by John Grafton.
     p. cm. — (Dover pictorial archive series)
  ISBN 0-486-42306-9 (pbk.)
    1. United States—History—Civil War, 1861–1865—Pictorial works. I. Grafton, John. II. Series.

E468.9 .C47 2003
973.7'022'2—dc21

                       2002074159

Book design by Carol Belanger Grafton

Manufactured in the United States of America
Dover Publications, Inc., 31 East 2nd Street, Mineola, N.Y. 11501

# CONTENTS

# INTRODUCTION

THE AMERICAN CIVIL WAR was a war of many "firsts." Among the most dramatic of these were the technological innovations that enabled the first wartime use of ironclad warships, machine guns, and the reconnaissance balloon. This was the first war in which the telegraph and the railroad played significant roles. It was also the first war of which there is an immense photographic record, and, by no means least significant, it was the first war to be covered on a regular basis by illustrated weekly newspapers.

In the relatively placid 1850s, two major American publishing enterprises, both based in New York City, Harper Brothers and their rival firm, named for its founder Frank Leslie, each began publishing a weekly newspaper. Newspapers themselves were not new in America in the middle of the nineteenth century. They had already played a huge role in the culture of the colonial period, and in the political and civic life of the new American republic. The power of the press was well understood by the Founding Fathers. George Washington never actually delivered his famous Farewell Address as a speech—he just sent it to the newspapers and in a few weeks it was widely available in all of the original thirteen states and beyond. What was new in the 1850s, when *Harper's Weekly*, which modestly subtitled itself "A Journal of Civilization," and *Frank Leslie's Illustrated Newspaper* began operations, was that through the medium of wood engraving, the newspaper's text could now be supplemented with pictures.

During the few short years between the establishment of these first American weekly illustrated newspapers and the start of the Civil War, those texts and pictures represented a mild and varied cross section of the interests of the reading public of that era. Depicted in these illustrations were crowded city street scenes, pastoral views of scenic wonders, sailing ships and steamships, fashion illustrations, the homes of leading citizens, portraits of European royalty, botanical and zoological curiosities, thoroughbred horses and new and improved carriages, inventions of all kinds, schools and prisons, stores and factories—just about anything and everything. The bombardment of Fort Sumter on April 12, 1861, changed all of that. From that time on, these illustrated weeklies had a definitive subject and focus—a war for the survival of the nation and control over its political and philosophical destiny. This bitter struggle was occurring only a few hundred miles from the center of New York City's printing and publishing industries. For the next four years, the war was really the only story, and the editors, writers, and illustrators of the weeklies understood that. Aspects of their coverage could be criticized, were in fact criticized both at the time and since, but no one could deny that in their pages this great story was fully covered.

For the purposes of this volume, a small sampling of the illustrations that appeared in these illustrated weeklies have been used to create a condensed narrative history of the Civil War, which is, of necessity, also a history of the way the war was portrayed to the readers of *Harper's* and *Leslie's*. What exactly did the readers of *Harper's* receive for their six cents a week ($3.00 a year in advance)? Sixteen large folio pages with a lot of text, including many regular features that were continued from an earlier era such as serialized fiction stories; and many, many wood engraved portraits of politicians, statesmen, captains, colonels, generals and admirals, staring off the pages in their cumbersome uniforms, swords at their sides; shipping news and maps of varying degrees of accuracy; and, above all else, pictures of the action.

Quality improved as the war continued. In the early days, the idea of covering a war was new, and action illustrations were certainly drawn, engraved, and published that were based on sketchy accounts at best. Sometimes, these engravings were based only on the artists' vivid imaginations. Pictures were common of soldiers proceeding into battle in impeccable uniforms in impossibly precise formations, rows upon rows of bayonets held at exactly the same angle. Pictures were also published of battles at remote locations, such as Shiloh, which were certainly pulled more or less out of the air because no artist was actually there to draw them. But as time and the war went on and the ranks of the artist-correspondents were gradually filled by competent professionals who wanted to tell their story accurately, the pictures published came to have a greater sense of reality. This volume contains the work of many anonymous artists and some who were well known, from Winslow Homer, who created some memorable Civil War pictures for *Harper's Weekly* and then went on to other artistic pursuits, to artist-correspondents such as Alfred Waud and Theodore Davis, who had longer careers working in this medium. Was it ever possible through the medium of wood engraving to capture what it was really like for armies of tens of thousands of soldiers attacking and counterattacking across farms and rivers, open fields and dense woods? Probably not, but it doesn't detract from the significance of this material to realize that this is essentially a book about the way in which the American Civil War was portrayed at the time. We can start to understand something about the war and its period when we understand something about how the civilians then at home, in New York City offices, small Connecticut farms, and fishing villages on the Maine coast, got their news about it, week after week, year after year.

This collection reprints a selection of the pictures these civilians saw. The pictures themselves represent the attitudes of many at the time. Although intense scenes of hand-to-hand combat with swords and bayonets were frequently depicted, we now know after almost a century and a half of research and tens of thousands of books and articles (the American Civil War is certainly one of the most written-about events in world history) that hand-to-hand combat was not the norm in the Civil War, and battlefield deaths due to bayonets were rare. However, those scenes made for good pictures, and more than just good pictures, they also had propaganda value. The illustrated weeklies were Northern papers with a strong Union bias. Though writers and commentators in the North certainly responded to the gallantry and brilliance of the great Confederate generals—Lee, Stonewall Jackson, and others—many of these illustrations have a pro-Union propaganda subtext. The Confederacy didn't have an illustrated paper of their own; if such a paper did exist, it would be fascinating to compare its coverage to that of some of the same incidents as reported in *Harper's* and *Leslie's*.

The photographers of the Civil War and their priceless legacy are justly famous, but the cumbersome technology of the time made it impossible then to take action photographs while battles were raging. The photographic remains of the Civil War are views of places where great battles took place, portraits of participants, and the carnage the battles left behind. Spend an afternoon with a thousand Civil War photographs and you come away with an idea of the desolate immensity of the events of that era, and that this was a war in which over six hundred thousand soldiers actually died on the battlefield—an idea that you can't get from the wood engravings that were published in *Harper's Weekly* and *Frank Leslie's Illustrated Newspaper.* But spend an afternoon with these wood engravings of battles and fighting on horseback, and warships ramming each other and huge mortar attacks and soldiers in camp and on the march, and you come away with a feeling for the way news of this war circulated at the time, before photographs could be reproduced for mass circulation, a feeling that you don't get from the still photographs of the dead lying on the field at Antietam. Two sides of the same coin. We're fortunate to have them both.

The secession crisis which led to the start of the Civil War followed decades of political and ideological conflict between Northern and Southern states over the future of slavery in America. As the two regions developed during the country's first century, the differences between them were profound. The South's agrarian economy was based on one major crop, cotton, produced on large plantations by slave labor. In the North were smaller farms that employed free labor in a growing urban manufacturing and industrial econ-

omy. The battle over the issue of slavery was simultaneously economic, political, and philosophical. In the years leading up to the conflict, debate was focused mostly on whether slavery would be allowed in new, western states. For a time even after the start of the war, Lincoln and his moderate supporters denied any intention to eliminate slavery where it had always existed. Increasingly, however, the growing impetus in the North for total abolition, which just a few decades previously had been the cause of an ideological fringe movement, took center stage. Less than halfway through the war, following the bloody battle of Antietam, Lincoln issued the preliminary version of the Emancipation Proclamation, which stated that all slaves residing in states that were in conflict with the Union would be freed as of January 1, 1863. The philosophical conflict over slavery was inseparable from the ongoing heated debate over states' rights. Would the federal government be able to dictate to the individual states on these matters, or did the states have the right to decide these fundamental questions for themselves? When debate and discussion failed to resolve these great issues, the country went to war with itself.

The immediate crisis was sparked by the election of the antislavery candidate of the new Republican Party, Abraham Lincoln, to the presidency in November 1860. Lincoln received 40 percent of the popular vote in a three-way race, and 180 out of 303 electoral votes. On December 20, 1860, South Carolina became the first Southern state to secede from the Union, followed during the next two months by Mississippi, Florida, Alabama, Georgia, Louisiana, and Texas. Following the attack on Fort Sumter in April, these seven states were joined by Virginia, Arkansas, Tennessee, and North Carolina. The eleven seceding states formed the Confederate States of America. The first seven Confederate states met at a convention in Montgomery, Alabama, in February 1861, adopted the Confederate Constitution, and named Jefferson Davis provisional president of the Confederacy until elections could be held at some future time. Following the secession of Virginia in April, Richmond was named the Confederate capital. This choice was to have profound consequences, guaranteeing that for as long as it lasted, much of the conflict would be fought over the area of northeastern Virginia between Washington and Richmond. For four very long years, increasingly massive armies would face each other there in a devastating minuet of attack and defense, threat and counterthreat, aimed at each other's capital cities, less than 150 miles apart. Finally, only in the last week of the war, Richmond would fall to Grant's army. When Lincoln received the news of Lee's surrender at Appomattox a few days later, he was in fact in Richmond, surveying the rubble of the Confederate capital.

JOHN GRAFTON

# 1861
## *Fort Sumter to Port Royal*

WHEN ABRAHAM LINCOLN was inaugurated on March 4, 1861, he reiterated his long-held position that despite his personal opposition to slavery, he had no plans to end it in states where it already existed, but that he would oppose secession by the Confederate states. At that time there was still hope — rapidly fading, but still hope — in many areas North and South that the crisis could still be resolved without warfare. Six weeks into Lincoln's presidency, that hope would be extinguished by a barrage of cannon fire across the harbor of Charleston, South Carolina. The battle lines came into focus quickly. Four states in which slavery was then still legal — Delaware, Kentucky, Maryland, and Missouri — remained in the Union, the combined effect of divided loyalties among their citizens, military pressure, and deft political maneuvering. Shortly after the start of the Civil War, the western counties of Virginia rejected secession and were finally admitted to the Union as the state of West Virginia in 1863. At the start of the Civil War, the eleven Confederate states had a combined population of 9 million, including almost 4 million slaves. The twenty-one Union states had a population of over 20 million and vastly more industrial capacity.

The fighting began with the attack on Fort Sumter in Charleston Harbor at 4:30 A.M. on April 12, 1861. Surrounded by Confederate artillery, and with supplies and ammunition running low and no way to receive reinforcements, Fort Sumter fell to the Confederacy the following day. On April 15, Lincoln issued a proclamation calling for 75,000 militiamen from the Northern states to defend the Union and summoning a special session of Congress for July 4. At that session, Congress authorized the expansion of the Union Army by 500,000 men. Some weeks of minor and inconclusive military action after Fort Sumter were followed by the Union debacle at the First Battle of Bull Run in July. Pushed by popular and political pressure to take decisive action, the Union command under Gen. Winfield Scott ordered an attack on Confederate troops at Manassas Junction, Virginia, near a small creek called Bull Run, twenty-five miles southwest of Washington. The Union troops, under Gen. Irvin McDowell, had some success in the early hours following their initial attack on July 21, but Confederate reinforcements arrived — some by railroad, then a novelty in military planning — in time to turn the tide and enable the Confederates under Gen. Joseph E. Johnston and Gen. P. G. T. Beauregard to send McDowell's troops in a chaotic retreat back toward Washington. On July 27, Lincoln named Gen. George B. McClellan to replace McDowell as commander of the Department of the Potomac. Later on, in November 1861, McClellan would succeed the elderly Scott as general-in-chief of the entire Union army. The major effect of Bull Run in the North was to bring home the sobering realization that the conflict would be long and bloody.

The first summer of the war saw the Union establish a naval blockade of the long Confederate coastline, requiring a massive buildup that involved building new ships as well as converting existing civilian ships for military use. In a few months, the Union blockade of Southern shipping began to exhibit an effect much quicker than might have seemed possible at the outset. One response by the Confederacy was the use of smaller, faster ships that were able to sometimes — but only sometimes — outrun the blockades. Union naval efforts were aided by the capture of Port Royal and the Sea Islands of South Carolina in November 1861 and the establishment there of a naval base to provide support for the blockade. Also in November, the Union avoided an international crisis and possible war with England over the seizure by the U.S. Navy on the high seas of two Confederate diplomats on their way to confer with the British government. Bowing to British diplomatic pressure and releasing the Confederate diplomats, Lincoln simply commented, "One war at a time." Eighteen sixty-one came to an end with casualties mounting on both sides and no light at the end of the tunnel.

1

2

*2 | 1861: Fort Sumter to Port Royal*

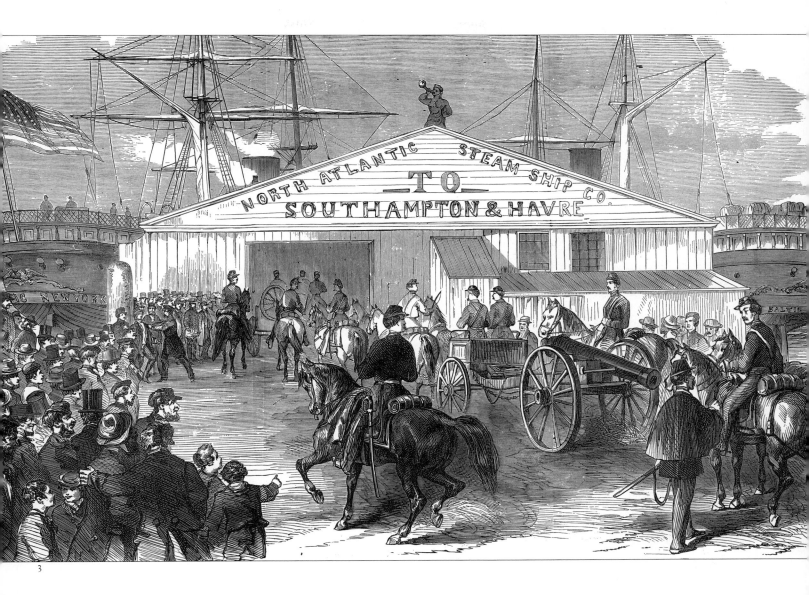

3

1. Charleston Harbor was the scene of military action even before the Civil War officially began. This picture illustrates Confederate batteries on Morris Island firing on the *Star of the West* on January 9, 1861, when the ship, a chartered merchant steamer commissioned by the federal government to bring reinforcements to Fort Sumter, arrived off Charleston with 200 soldiers and supplies for the garrison. Damaged by the shelling from these guns, the Union ship was forced to withdraw without landing her troops at Fort Sumter. The *Star of the West* had an unlucky history as the Civil War continued. She was captured by Confederate forces off Matagorda Bay, Texas, in April 1861, and in 1863, was intentionally sunk to serve as an obstruction to Union ships near Fort Pemberton on the Tallahatchie River in Mississippi.

2. Soldiers of New York's Seventh Regiment marching down Broadway a few days after the surrender of Fort Sumter in April 1861. Responding to a special request from President Lincoln, the New York Seventh was on duty in Washington by late April. The Seventh served at many Union camps, especially in Maryland,

during the next two years, and was back in New York in time to see action during the draft riots in July 1863. Their statutory period of service having been completed, the regiment was mustered out on July 21, 1863.

3. Preparations for the embarkation of Union soldiers heading south from the Collins Line Dock at the foot of Canal Street in New York in early April 1861. The press reported that a total of 858 soldiers shipped out on the *Atlantic*, the *Baltic*, and the *Illinois* at the New York dock, where, before the war, transatlantic steamships received their passengers for Southampton and Le Havre.

*Overleaf*: 4. Inside one of the Confederate floating batteries in Charleston Harbor with Fort Sumter in the distance during the bombardment of April 12–13, 1861. The battery was well stocked with ammunition and supplies for the battle, which must have seemed inevitable once South Carolina left the Union in December 1860.

5

6

LATEST FROM
CHARLESTON
SUMTER ON FIRE!!
REBELS FIRING ON
THE BURNING FORT!!

7

5. Sgt. Hart restoring the Stars and Stripes to the ramparts of Fort Sumter in Charleston Harbor on April 13, 1861, during the last hours of the bombardment, which signaled the start of the Civil War.

The Civil War began at 4:30 A.M. on April 12, 1861, when 43 Confederate guns encircling Fort Sumter, named for a Revolutionary War patriot, opened fire on the Union fort. The bombardment followed several days of ultimately unsuccessful negotiations to secure the surrender of the indefensible fort by the South Carolina authorities, who, following the secession of their state from the Union, now claimed sovereignty over it. Fort Sumter was under the command of Major Robert Anderson who was unwilling to comply with the demands of his Confederate counterpart (and former artillery student at West Point), Gen. P. G. T. Beauregard, commander of the Confederate forces in Charleston. With only enough food for a few weeks, and no way to land reinforcements or supplies, the outcome of the Confederate bombardment was a foregone conclusion. After a few hours of shelling, Anderson's forces returned fire, the first shot launched by Anderson's second-in-command, Captain Abner Doubleday. However, with their supply of ammunition low, and many of their guns in unprotected locations on Sumter's upper tier and positioned to fire out to sea and therefore useless in this battle, the return fire from the fort had little real effect.

Once the fort's garrison flag was shot down on the second day of the bombardment, several soldiers, among them Sgt. Hart, restored a smaller storm flag (considerably smaller than the flag shown in this illustration) to its place. The restored flag survived the rest of the two-day battle. When Anderson finally surrendered after 33 hours of shelling, the fort was heavily damaged, but no soldiers on either side had been killed or badly wounded. As part of the surrender agreement, however, the Confederates agreed to allow a military salute to the flag, which was still flying. During this exercise, which began at 2 P.M. on April 14, an accidental explosion killed one of the Union soldiers. The remaining Union soldiers, carrying their tattered flag, marched out of the fort and boarded a boat which ferried them to Union ships waiting outside the harbor to take them north.

6. The 10-inch Columbiad cannon was the only gun at Fort Sumter potentially capable of firing a shell far enough (3.3 miles, just about its maximum range) to hit the city of Charleston. However, Major Anderson and his officers decided not to fire on the city during the bombardment of the fort. The hundred-pound shells that the Columbiad could launch remained unused during the two-day battle.

7. A newspaper poster on a Northern street corner gives the news from Charleston in April 1861. It is one of the ironies of Civil War history that its first battle was fought over a minor fort of no military significance and ended without casualties on either side. While the loss of the fort had no military importance, the symbolic loss was deeply felt in the North and brought home in an immediate way the fact that the war between the states, which had been feared and anticipated for so long, was indeed a reality.

8

8. The Sixth Massachusetts Regiment leaving the Jersey City Railroad depot on their way to defend Washington on April 18, 1861. At the start of the Civil War, the United States Army numbered only 16,000 men, and President Lincoln issued an urgent call to the individual Union states to provide 75,000 volunteers for 90 days' service in defense of Washington. As part of this military buildup to protect the capital, the Massachusetts Sixth, which had been organized only a few months earlier, had arrived in New York by train, marched across the city, and then were ferried across the Hudson by boat to board trains for Washington at Jersey City.

9. On the following day, April 19, the 800-man Massachusetts Sixth was attacked with flying paving stones and handgun fire on Pratt Street in Baltimore. They were met and attacked by a pro-Confederate crowd while marching from the station where their train had just arrived from Jersey City. The pitched battle on the

Baltimore streets saw the first casualties of the war in the North. Four soldiers of the Massachusetts Regiment were killed in the riot along with approximately twelve civilians. While Maryland was technically a Union state, there was considerable pro-Southern sentiment among its citizens.

10. The Billy Wilson Zouaves, a colorful regiment formed by a New York politician, swearing their allegiance to the Union flag at New York's Tammany Hall in late April 1861. Col. Wilson is pictured in the center with the flag in one hand and a sword in the other. This 1,200-man regiment from one of New York's rougher neighborhoods left for the South a few days later. Wilson's Zouaves saw action in Florida and Louisiana before being mustered out when their term expired in 1863. Forty-six enlisted members didn't make it back; 14 were killed in action and 32 succumbed to disease.

9

10

11

12

**11.** The start of the Civil War immediately affected life in every area of the country, even those far removed from the fighting. It wasn't all patriotic parades and celebrations. This 1861 illustration shows Confederate prisoners being transported to Fort Lafayette in New York Harbor. The fort, built on a small rock island in the narrows opposite Fort Hamilton between Long Island and the lower end of Staten Island, was used to house prisoners captured by Union forces beginning with Confederate POWs taken in West Virginia by McClellan's army in the summer of 1861. Hundreds of prisoners were held there in miserable conditions, equally as bad as those in any other Civil War prison, North or South, for the duration of the war. Overcrowding, bad food, little or no health care, poor sanitation, and rampant disease earned Fort Lafayette the designation as "the American Bastille." The last POWs were released from Fort Lafayette only some months after the war came to an end in 1865.

**12.** Forging iron for gun carriages at Watervliet Arsenal, West Troy, New York. Watervliet, the oldest arsenal in America, still in use in 2003, was founded by Congress in 1813. During the Civil War, vast amounts of ammunition of many kinds were produced there. Artillery barrels were produced by outside contractors, but the Arsenal constructed the carriages for them, as illustrated here. During the 1863 draft riots, the city of Troy, across the Hudson from Watervliet, was looted by a huge mob, but the Arsenal's workers and 65 regular army soldiers stationed there kept the Arsenal from becoming a target of mob discontent.

**13.** In the early days of the Civil War, attacks on Washington were greatly feared but never materialized. Here the Eighth Massachusetts Volunteers set up camp in the rotunda of the Capital in April 1861.

**14.** Lacking the manpower to protect or remove valuable ships from the indefensible Union shipyard at Norfolk, Virginia, the Union intentionally burned several ships on April 20, 1861, in an attempt to prevent their falling into Confederate hands as the Civil War began. This detail from a larger panorama shows the U.S.S. *Pawnee* on the left, and the U.S.S. *Pennsylvania*. The *Pennsylvania* was one of several Union ships set on fire and left at Norfolk. The *Pawnee* was one of a few that escaped the destruction at Norfolk, and was successfully sailed to Washington to assist in the city's defense. Despite Union efforts to destroy the Norfolk Yard, guns and other vital material fell into Confederate hands there, as did the Union dry dock and industrial plant, which proved to be of major importance to the Southern war effort in the early months of the war.

13

14

15

**15.** In the first months of the war, much of the military activity centered on Washington and the nearby Virginia countryside. Here, in the days leading up to the First Battle at Bull Run, a Union foraging party returns to camp near Annandale Chapel, Virginia, seven miles from Alexandria and ten from Washington. Civil War armies carried their guns and ammunition with them, and supplemented these with whatever they could capture along the way. For food, however, they often had to rely on what they could find wherever they happened to be.

**16.** The skirmish at Philippi, Virginia, a minor Union victory in the early summer of 1861, an inconclusive prologue to the First Battle of Bull Run. Union troops under the command of Cols. E. Dumont and B. F. Kelly carried out a two-pronged assault against a Confederate brigade occupying the town of Philippi on June 3. The Confederate brigade was routed and retreated toward Huttonsville in the first meaningful land action in the Eastern theater. Kelly was wounded in the action, which saw no more than 30 casualties on both sides.

**17.** Lt. Tompkins of B Company, U.S. Dragoons, leading a charge into Fairfax Courthouse, Virginia, against 1,500 Confederates on June 1, 1861. Tomkins' horse was shot from under him while the Union forces fought their way through the town and took 17 prisoners. This minor skirmish at Fairfax Courthouse saw the first Confederate officer casualty of the Civil War, Captain John Quincy Marr.

16

17

18

19

20

**18.** The Battle of Rich Mountain, Virginia, July 11–13, 1861, another prologue to Bull Run. Maj. Gen. George McClellan had taken command of Union forces in western Virginia in June 1861. McClellan's troops and those of Brig. Gen. William S. Rosecrans fought a significant but outnumbered Confederate force at Rich Mountain in July. This victory was a major factor in securing for McClellan command of the entire Army of the Potomac a few weeks later, after the debacle at Bull Run.

**19.** Advancing on foot at Rich Mountain. This victory secured Union control of part of northwestern Virginia, and its crucial railroad, the Baltimore and Ohio, for the remainder of the war.

**20.** At Rich Mountain, the Thirteenth Indiana Regiment captures a cannon. Skirmishing with a Confederate force (holding the log cabin pictured here), the Thirteenth Indiana first took the cabin, then mounted a bayonet charge, capturing the cannon and taking prisoners.

21

22

23

**21.** The first major battle of the Civil War, the First Battle of Bull Run, took place in Virginia on July 21, 1861. It pitted the Union force under McDowell against the Confederate army under Johnston and Beauregard. Note the artist-correspondent seated in the foreground sketching the scene in front of him while officers and civilians outside the range of combat watch the action unfolding through binoculars as artillery and infantry reinforcements move up beside them. Bull Run was the first major battle fought by the armies in Virginia and the size of it dwarfed previous action. To the Union side, it reinforced the idea that the war was going to be long and costly. Rich Mountain, only days earlier, had been an important battle, but had cost only an estimated total of less than 400 casualties. Bull Run brought almost 5,000 casualties—dead and wounded combined—with more losses on the Union side than on the Confederacy's.

The untested and inexperienced Union Army left Washington to take on the equally unprepared Confederates standing ready at Bull Run, a strategically important location as a railroad junction, on July 16. The armies met on the 21st. The Union Army had the advantage early on, but Confederate reinforcements, one brigade of which arrived by rail from the Shenandoah Valley, turned the tide, breaking the Union right flank, and sending the Union Army back toward Washington in a chaotic retreat. Though the Confederate forces were too exhausted and disorganized to pursue their advantage, the devastated Union Army reached the Capital on the 22nd, and the Confederate victory was clear. The careers of two of the war's major personalities were deeply affected by Bull Run. On the Union side, McClellan was given command of the Army of the Potomac, and on the Confederate side, the resolute leadership of the brilliant Gen. Thomas J. Jackson forever earned him the nickname "Stonewall." Sixty thousand soldiers had been involved on both sides, and nothing like it had ever been seen

before on the North American continent. When it was over, everyone—from President Lincoln to the lowest-ranking soldier—knew then that the war was not going to be won that summer.

**22.** A Confederate officer being escorted back to the Confederate lines after a failed peace mission in the days leading up to Bull Run. There were several unsuccessful meetings between representatives of both sides in the early weeks of the war.

**23.** Another image of Bull Run. As in many contemporary Civil War illustrations, the regular formations of soldiers on the attack pictured here, with rows of bayonets poised at exactly the same angle, are idealized constructions. However, the confusion and devastation of hand-to-hand combat under clouds of artillery smoke and over the bodies of dead horses seems real enough even in this picture. Bull Run established a pattern that would be repeated many times. After one side would win a victory during a long day of fighting, nightfall and darkness would bring a forced end to hostilities. Night was reserved for burying the dead and searching the battlefield with torches, keeping an eye out for the occasional sniper while looking for any soldiers who might still be alive. The victors would be too exhausted to follow up any advantage, while the defeated side would retreat into surrounding country. By the next morning, the defeated armies couldn't be pursued effectively, and the potentially crushing blow would never be delivered. Both sides would then regroup and fight again, sooner or later, be it down the road, in the next village, through the next abandoned farm, or somewhere on the other side of the river. In the end, the Union's superior numbers proved decisive, and the long war of attrition came stumbling to a finish almost four years after this first meeting at Bull Run.

24

25

26

**24.** The New York Twenty-first Volunteers manning a Union artillery battery at Fort Runyon, Virginia, commanding the road to Alexandria in 1861. Fort Runyon was constructed at the start of the war to protect the Long Bridge over the Potomac.

**25.** A Confederate artillery battery practicing with a Sawyer gun at Sewell's Point, Virginia. Very early in the war there was some skirmishing between Union gunboats and the Sewell's Point batteries as part of the Union effort to enforce the blockade of Hampton Roads, but no major battles. Though attacked many times, the Sewell's Point batteries were never captured. They were abandoned when Confederate forces evacuated Norfolk on May 10, 1862.

**26.** The aftermath of Bull Run brought the reality of the war home to the North, in case there was any doubt. Here, wounded Union soldiers captured at Bull Run are pictured heading home on board a ship off Hampton Roads, Virginia, in October 1861. The Confederate authorities, lacking facilities to deal with wounded prisoners, returned these soldiers to Union authorities under a flag of truce. The U.S. steamer *Express* met the Confederate steamer *Northumberland* under truce twelve miles above Newport News, and took back 57 prisoners captured by the Confederates at Bull Run.

27

27. Destruction of cannons and gun carriages at the Confederate arsenal at Beaufort, South Carolina, by a Union raiding party off the gunboat *Seneca* on November 14, 1861. The *Seneca* was a 691-ton steam gunboat, built at the Jeremiah Simonson shipyard in New York City. Launched on August 27, 1861, it was commissioned in October 1861 to take part in the complete Union blockade of Southern ports, which started after the surrender of Fort Sumter. In addition to the action at Beaufort pictured here, the *Seneca* took part in the capture of Port Royal, also in November 1861, and in many blockading operations throughout the war. The *Seneca* was decommissioned at Norfolk, Virginia, in 1865.

28. Another aspect of the war at sea in 1861. A contemporary artist's rendering depicts a device deployed by the Confederates that attempted to damage the Union fleet in the Potomac. The device was discovered by Capt. Rudd of the Union steamer *Resolute* near Aquia Creek in early July 1861, as it was floating

toward the Union ship *Pawnee*. It consisted of two 80-gallon watertight oil casks connected by rope and buoyed by squares of cork. The underwater bombs were made of boiler iron containers filled with powder, held at a depth of six feet, and were connected to above-water fuses by long tubes. The idea was to light the fuses and float the device toward an enemy ship. When the flame reached the powder, hopefully as the floating bomb reached the unsuspecting ship, the bomb would detonate, putting a hole in the target ship at the water line. In this case, it didn't reach the target.

29. A shell explodes on the cutter belonging to the Union steamer *Niagara* on November 3, 1861. A party from the *Niagara* was returning to their ship after setting the Confederate brig *Nonsuch* on fire near New Orleans. A shell hit the cutter, damaging the small boat and throwing two officers into the water. Another cutter dispatched from the *Niagara* rescued the party.

28

29

30

31

32

**30.** Like Fort Sumter, Fort Pickens, Florida, in 1861 was the scene of memorable events during the first year of the Civil War. Built in 1829–34 on the western tip of Santa Rosa Island to protect Pensacola Harbor, Fort Pickens had been unused and deserted since the Mexican War of the 1840s. As the secession crisis deepened early in 1861, Lt. Adam J. Slemmer, commanding officer of the small federal garrison at Fort Barrancas, located on the mainland across from Fort Pickens, decided that the unused fort on Santa Rosa would be more defensible than Barrancas. This belief was confirmed on January 8, 1861, when Slemmer's men repelled an irregular assault on Barrancas, firing what could be considered the first shots by Union forces in the Civil War. The war didn't start, though, over these shots, or over the *Star of the West* incident in Charleston Harbor the same month. Lt. Slemmer, however, didn't wait—he spiked the guns at Barrancas, destroyed 20,000 pounds of powder at Fort McRee a few miles away, also on the mainland, and transferred his approximately 80 troops to Fort Pickens.

**31.** Inside one of the ten casement batteries at Fort Pickens. Pickens had been built using slave labor, with over 22 million bricks and turned out to be, as it was designed, virtually impregnable to attack. Col. William H. Chase of the Corps of Army Engineers had supervised the construction. Ironically, Chase was later appointed by the state of Florida to command the troops ordered to seize Fort Pickens for the South, but this proved impossible to do. Fort Pickens remained in Union hands for the duration of the Civil War, denying the Confederate Navy the best harbor on the Gulf of Mexico and providing immense assistance to the Union Navy in carrying out the blockade of Southern shipping.

**32.** Landing supplies for Fort Pickens during the reinforcement of the fort by Union ships in April 1861. Protected by the guns aboard the ship that brought them, the U.S.S. *Powhatan*, 600 soldiers also arrived to reinforce the fort. Transporting horses from supply ships even a little way out at sea provided some interesting logistical puzzles that were solved in a variety of ways, as illustrated here.

**33.** The Battle for Port Royal—Landing of United States Troops at Fort Walker after the bombardment on November 7, 1861. In April 1861, the United States Navy had only forty-two ships in commission. Only a few of these were immediately available to try to enforce the blockade of Southern ports that President Lincoln proclaimed a few days after the surrender of Fort Sumter. As part of the naval buildup necessitated by the task of patrolling the almost three thousand miles of Southern coastline, the Union command decided to try to capture the entrance to Port Royal, South Carolina, and to establish there a naval base where their coal-burning ships could refuel and head for needed repairs. Port Royal was selected as the preferred target for this initiative because its deep water and wide channel would permit easier access to larger ships than some other potential locations. The selection of Port Royal was urged by influential navy men who saw its significance, including Assistant Secretary of the Navy Gustavus V. Fox and Flag Officer Samuel F. Du Pont. In early November 1861, the two Confederate forts at Port Royal—Forts Walker and Beauregard—were abandoned by the Confederates following a four-hour naval bombardment, and the Union forces landed unopposed, as illustrated here.

**34.** A view from the interior of Fort Walker, Port Royal, South Carolina, during the bombardment by the Union fleet on November 7, 1861. The large Union fleet circled in the water off the fort, built on a bluff eight feet above the high-water line, each ship firing in turn as it came opposite the fort. The Union ships *Wabash*, *Bienville*, and *Susquehanna* were ultimately able to get within six hundred yards of the fort, a distance from which they were able to inflict major damage. When the Confederate forts were abandoned, over 12,000 Union soldiers were landed by a large flotilla of small boats. For many of the Union soldiers involved in the landing, this was their first experience of battle, and the devastation they found inside the abandoned forts, the dead and wounded Confederate defenders, made a lasting impression. On a broader, more strategic level, the Union success at Port Royal represented something of a morale-boosting turning point. It followed a summer of defeats on land that had started at Bull Run in Virginia in July, and continued at Wilson's Creek in Missouri in August and at Ball's Bluff in Virginia in October.

35

36

37

**35.** Union losses in the summer of 1861 were not confined to Virginia. This illustration shows a scene from the war in Missouri in that summer, the charge of the First Iowa Regiment, under General Nathaniel Lyon, at the Battle of Wilson's Creek, twelve miles southwest of Springfield, Missouri, on August 10, 1861. The press described it as a bloody battle between 5,200 Federals and 22,000 Confederates, which ended in a Confederate victory. The First Iowa charged against superior numbers and were routed. Gen. Lyon, wounded and having had his horse killed underneath him, mounted another horse and was killed soon after. At the end of the day, a total of over 2,000 were dead or wounded on both sides. The defeated Union forces retreated toward Springfield. The Confederate forces, now exhausted, were not organized enough to pursue immediately, but the battle had important consequences, both militarily and politically. After Wilson's Creek, the Missouri State Guard, spearhead of the Confederate victory there, regrouped to push north toward Lexington and another crucial success. In October, Missouri Governor Claiborne Fox Johnson called a rump convention at Neosho, where an ordinance of secession was passed. Wilson's Creek gave the Confederates solid control of southwestern Missouri.

**36.** The defense of Lexington, September 1861. Following their victory at Wilson's Creek, the Missouri State Guard, commanded by Maj. Gen. Sterling Price, marched north toward Lexington to attack the 3,500-man Union garrison there. After skirmishing which began on September 13, Price wisely waited for ammunition, reinforcements, and other supplies, and then began an assault on the fortified Union position on the 18th. This resulted in a request for surrender terms by the Union Commander, Col. James A. Mulligan, on the afternoon of the 20th. The fall of this Union stronghold reinforced Confederate control in the Missouri Valley west of Arrow Rock. The battle had been unusually one-sided—Union forces surrendered after losing over 1,700 men while the Confederates had only about a hundred casualties. At a crucial point on the 20th, some of Price's forces advanced behind improvised mobile breastworks made of hemp, putting themselves in good position for a final assault. As a result, Lexington is sometimes known as "The Battle of the Hemp Bales."

**37.** Cooking in camp; the camp kitchen of the Fremont Dragoons, a unit under Gen. John Charles Fremont, commander of the Union's Department of the West, at Tipton, Missouri, near Jefferson City and Sedalia. This was an important camp, as it was located near the railroad that passed through Jefferson City and ended, at that time, in Sedalia.

38

**38.** The war in the west in 1861. Camp Zagonyi, the camp of Fremont's army, near Wheatland, Missouri, in October 1861. The Grand Army of the West camped at this location after a fifteen-mile march from Tipton in October 1861. Camp Zagonyi, on the open prairie, was very different from the rolling, wooded Virginia countryside where much of the earlier action in 1861 had occurred. It was named for Major Charles Zagonyi, a well-known member of Fremont's staff and commander of a special advance unit known as Fremont's Body Guards. Zagonyi's unit spear-headed the victory of Fremont's troops at Springfield, Missouri, in late October 1861, the only Union victory in southwestern Missouri in the opening year of the war.

**39.** The battle at Springfield, Missouri, on October 25, 1861, the second charge against the Confederates by Major Zagonyi's troops. Zagonyi's Body Guards, an elite unit of 200 soldiers, and affiliated units advanced on Springfield in late October ahead of Fremont's main army. Based on information gathered from a captured foraging party, Zagonyi's Guards launched an attack on a larger Confederate encampment, and took Springfield on October 25. Fearing a coun-terattack, Zagonyi didn't stay at Springfield, but Fremont's main army returned a few days later and occupied the town.

The victory at Springfield came too late to save Fremont's position in the Union military hierarchy. Lincoln had appoint-ed the widely popular Fremont to command the Department of the West only in May 1861, under pressure from antislavery Republicans who saw Fremont, a bitter opponent of slavery and a former presidential candidate, as their spokesman. Ensconced with his new command in St. Louis, military success eluded Fremont from the start as his forces in Missouri suffered several defeats including the debacle at Wilson's Creek in August. When Fremont issued a proclamation declaring martial law in Missouri and ordered that secessionists' property be confiscated and their slaves emancipated, Lincoln tried unsuccessfully to get Fremont to at least modify his order. As a result, the presi-dent removed him from his command and revoked the famous proclamation the same week as the belated victory of Zagonyi's troops and Fremont's main army at Springfield. Fremont was never able to recapture a position of major influence in the Lincoln administration or in the Union high command.

**40.** Delaware Indians acting as scouts for the Federal Army in the West.

39

40

# 1862
## *Fort Henry to Fredericksburg*

As THE NEW YEAR began, Lincoln, anxious for some military success, issued an order authorizing the Union command to take aggressive action against the Confederacy. This order was ignored by General McClellan. In February, however, Grant scored major victories for the Union in western Tennessee, capturing Fort Henry on the 6th and Fort Donelson ten days later in the year's first major campaign. Nashville became the first Confederate state capital to be captured by Union forces. In March, Lincoln, increasingly impatient with McClellan, reorganized the Army of Virginia and relieved McClellan of supreme command, replacing him with Ambrose Burnside. McClellan was given command of the Army of the Potomac and ordered to advance on Richmond. McClellan's troops proceeded down the Potomac River and Chesapeake Bay from Washington to the peninsula which runs southeast of Richmond, bounded by the York River on the north and the James on the south, to begin an advance on the Confederate capital. This was the start of the ultimately unsuccessful Peninsular Campaign. Also in March, the Union Army scored a major victory at Pea Ridge/Elkhorn Tavern in Missouri, securing control of Missouri for the next two years, and the Union *Monitor* and Confederate *Virginia (Merrimack)* fought their legendary ironclad duel off Hampton Roads, Virginia.

In April, the Confederate States took up conscription to raise needed troops. On the 6th, 63,000 Union troops under Gen. Ulysses S. Grant met 40,000 Confederate soldiers at Shiloh in Tennessee. The Confederate Army had the advantage at the end of the first day, but Union reinforcements arrived during the night and fortunes turned the following day. When the battle was over, the Confederates retreated, but the Union Army was too exhausted to follow up, and 24,000 men were dead or wounded on both sides. This was the highest number of casualties in one battle than had occurred in all previous American wars combined up to that date. Pressured to replace Grant because of the heavy losses, Lincoln refused, saying, "I can't spare this man—he fights." On April 24, Flag Officer David Farragut led a flotilla of seventeen Union ships up the Mississippi and took New Orleans, the South's major seaport, for the Union. McClellan's Peninsular Campaign encountered strong opposition in their slow progress toward Richmond. Stonewall Jackson pushed the Union Army back in the Shenandoah Valley in late spring and early summer, and troops rushed to defend Washington, D.C. In a busy week between June 26 and July 2, a series of battles in Virginia, Mechanicsville, Gaines' Mill, Savage's Station, Frayser's Farm, and Malvern Hill brought the Peninsular Campaign to an end with the Confederates, now under Gen. Robert E. Lee, withdrawing to Richmond after having secured the city from McClellan's troops, and McClellan pointing his men back toward Washington. Despite a huge commitment of men and resources, the failure of the Peninsular Campaign was a major blow to Northern hopes of bringing the war to an end anytime soon.

In July, Major General Henry Halleck took overall command of the Union Army. In August, John Pope's Union troops were defeated at the Second Battle of Bull Run, and Harper's Ferry was lost to the Confederacy in September. Two days after losing men and vital supplies at Harper's Ferry, McClellan caught up with Lee's army on Antietam Creek near Sharpsburg, Maryland. The Battle of Antietam on September 17 was one of the war's bloodiest, with nearly 5,000 killed on both sides and almost 20,000 wounded. It was not totally decisive militarily, but Lee retreated to Virginia, leaving McClellan the *de facto* winner. In the aftermath of Antietam, France and England deferred action on recognizing the Confederacy, which would have been a major diplomatic blow to the Union. Lincoln issued the preliminary version of the Emancipation Proclamation on September 22, freeing all slaves in the Confederate states effective January 1, 1863. Heavy action continued throughout the fall, and the year ended with Union forces in Virginia, under Burnside now instead of McClellan, unable to dislodge the entrenched Confederate Army at Fredericksburg. A series of frontal assaults on the Confederate position at Fredericksburg cost the Union over 12,000 casualties, more than twice the Confederate total, and didn't produce a victory. An anonymous but widely quoted Union soldier summed up the futility, "We might as well have tried to take hell." Following Fredericksburg, Burnside was replaced by Joseph Hooker. Eighteen sixty-two came to an end with the South having successfully defended Richmond from McClellan and the North having kept Lee away from Washington, but with no resolution, military or otherwise, anywhere in sight.

41

**41.** A detail from a larger panorama showing some of the hand-to-hand combat on January 19, 1862, at Mill Springs on the Cumberland River near Jamestown, Kentucky. This illustration depicts the conflict between a Confederate force of 8,000 under Zollicoffer and Crittenden, and 4,000 Federal troops commanded by General George H. Thomas. At a crucial juncture, the Confederate general Zollicoffer mistook some Union troops for his own and was killed in action as a result. His death left part of the Confederate lines without direction and Union reinforcements arrived in time to take the victory. Combined with the losses of Forts Henry and Donelson in Tennessee the following month, Mill Springs was a major loss to the Confederacy in Kentucky.

*Overleaf*: **42.** The explosion of a 42-pounder during the bombardment of Fort Henry. Eighteen sixty-two began with two related and crucial victories for Union forces, the captures of Fort Henry and Fort Donelson on the Tennessee and Cumberland Rivers. This gave the North control of two vital inland water routes for the movement of troops and equipment in the heart of the Confederate West.

Fort Henry, an earthen fort on the Tennessee River, was in danger of being flooded by the rising Tennessee River when troops under Brig. Gen. Ulysses S. Grant arrived on February 4 and 5. Grant established his divisions in two locations, one on the east bank of the Tennessee to prevent the garrison's escape, and the other on the high ground on the Kentucky side of the river, which rendered the fort strategically indefensible. The seven gunboats commanded by Flag Officer Andrew H. Foote began their bombardment of the fort, as illustrated here. The Confederate commander at Fort Henry, Brig. Gen. Lloyd Tilghman, quickly realized his position and, leaving artillery to hold off the Union gunboats as best they could, escorted his troops to Fort Donelson, ten miles away. When Tilghman returned to Fort Henry, the Union fleet had closed to within 400 yards of the fort, and Tilghman surrendered to the Union fleet.

43

**43.** Hand-to-hand fighting over a Union artillery battery at Fort Donelson on February 15, 1862. After Fort Henry surrendered on February 6, 1862, Grant immediately advanced to attack Fort Donelson, where the Confederate garrison from Fort Henry had retreated. The Confederate forces at Donelson failed in their attempt to break out through Grant's lines, and the 12,000-man garrison surrendered unconditionally on February 16. The fall of Forts Henry and Donelson, a disaster for the South, solidified Kentucky's position as a Union state and opened up Tennessee for an advance by the North via the Cumberland and Tennessee Rivers. The North's first major victory in the Civil War, coming almost a year after the attack on Fort Sumter, earned Grant both a promotion to major general and a new nickname. Toward the end of the battle, the Confederate General Simon Buckner inquired about the terms of a surrender, and Grant replied that only an unconditional and immediate surrender could be accepted. From then on, Ulysses S. Grant was known as "Unconditional Surrender Grant."

**44.** One of the victors at Fort Donelson, Union Gen. Lewis Wallace of the Eleventh Indiana Volunteers (Zouave Regiment) and his staff in an illustration from their West Virginia campaign. Wallace had served in the Mexican War in the 1840s, and then became a lawyer and politician in his native Indiana. His command did well at Fort Donelson, but his military reputation deteriorated after Shiloh, and despite some later successes, he never reached the top ranks of the Union command. He did serve, though, on the courts-martial held after the war that tried the Lincoln conspirators and Henry Wirz, the infamous commander of the Andersonville prison. Wallace is best remembered today as the prolific author of many novels, including one of the nineteenth-century's most popular works, *Ben Hur*.

*Overleaf*: **45.** Part of the early history of the Peninsular Campaign and one of the most memorable episodes in American naval history is the battle between the rival ironclads off Hampton Roads, Virginia, in March 1862. The first battle was between the Confederate iron-plated steamer *Virginia*, just arrived from her base at Norfolk, and the federal wooden sailing frigates *Cumberland* and *Congress*. Pictured here is the sinking of the *Cumberland* by a blow from the *Virginia* on Saturday, March 8, 1862. In addition to sinking the *Cumberland*, the *Virginia* succeeded in running the 50-gun *Congress* aground. The iron-sided *Virginia* proved relatively impervious to cannon fire from the conventional wooden-hulled Union ships she attacked that day. The *Virginia*, commanded by Captain Franklin Buchanan, was a scuttled 4,636-ton frigate, formerly the U.S.S. *Merrimack*. Burned and abandoned by the Union at the Gosport Navy Yard in Norfolk in 1861, before being converted to an ironclad by Confederate engineers, the *Merrimack* was rechristened the C.S.S. *Virginia*. (In some historical accounts, the *Merrimack*, which became the ironclad *Virginia*, is erroneously confused with a smaller Union gunboat, the *Merrimac*, which served as part of the East Coast Blockading Squadron and foundered in a gale off Florida in 1865.)

**46.** The following day, March 9, 1862, the naval battle at Hampton Roads took a different turn (illustrated here) as the Union ironclad *Monitor*, commanded by Lt. John Worden, arrived to engage the *Virginia* and prevent more damage by the Confederate ironclad to the conventional Union blockading fleet. It was a battle of heavyweights with contrasting styles—the *Virginia* carried more firepower, but was slower and less maneuverable than the *Monitor*. When the *Monitor* took a shot to her revolving tower, absorbing the blow and continuing to revolve, the Union officers gained confidence in their revolutionary new ship. The two ships fought to a draw in the first battle in history between ironclads, but eventually the *Virginia* retired from the conflict, so the *Monitor*'s efforts to protect her sister ships had to be considered a success. Later on, the *Virginia* ran aground and burned during the Confederate evacuation of Norfolk while the *Monitor* sank in a storm off Cape Hatteras. More than a century after their famous battle, the wreck of the *Monitor* was located and parts of the revolutionary ironclad, described at the time of the battle as "a Yankee raft with a cheese box on it," have now been salvaged.

*1862: Fort Henry to Fredericksburg* | 35

45

46

47

48

49

**47.** Ironclad technology proved so successful that both sides continued to develop it as the naval war progressed. The brilliant naval architect John Ericsson, responsible for the *Monitor*, turned his attention to even larger projects after the battle between the *Monitor* and the *Virginia*. The *Passaic*, illustrated here, was built by the Continental Iron Works in Greenport, New Jersey, under a subcontract from Ericsson, and launched on August 30, 1862. On December 26, she was being towed toward Beaufort, North Carolina, along with the *Monitor*, which sank in a storm off Cape Hatteras. The *Passaic* survived this storm. The *Passaic*, decommissioned at the Philadelphia Navy Yard in 1865, saw action in many campaigns during the last three years of the war.

**48.** A view of the interior of the *Passaic*'s turret gives an idea of the scale of the ironclads, the predecessors of the modern battleship. The huge 15-inch Dahlgren guns weighed over 40,000 pounds each and fired balls that weighed over 400 pounds. Despite the enormous weight of the guns and balls, the ingenious rotating mechanism of Ericsson's design enabled three sailors to operate one of these massive cannons from inside the turret.

**49.** The sinking of the *Monitor* in 1862.

50

51

40 / *1862: Fort Henry to Fredericksburg*

52

**50.** Shiloh on April 6, 1862, the charge and repulse of the Confederates at Peach Orchard.

Following the loss of Forts Henry and Donelson in February 1862, the Confederate commander, Gen. Albert Sidney Johnston, fell back to Corinth, Mississippi, virtually giving up Kentucky and western and central Tennessee. Corinth became Johnston's staging area while Grant gradually organized his 40,000-man Army of the Tennessee at Shiloh, also known as Pittsburg Landing, drilling his troops, many of which were raw recruits, and waiting to be joined there by the Army of the Ohio under Maj. Gen. Don Carlos Buell.

To the surprise of the Union command, Johnston attacked Grant's troops at Shiloh on April 6, 1862, and scored heavily in the early hours of the battle. A devastating loss to the Confederacy, however, was the battlefield death of Johnston, who was immediately replaced by his second-in-command, P. G. T. Beauregard. The Union forces held and were supported in time by the arrival of Buell's troops. Beauregard, unaware of Buell's arrival, launched a new attack on April 7, but, with his troops now badly outnumbered, was forced back. Realizing he couldn't win at Shiloh, Beauregard ordered a retreat back to Corinth. On the 8th, Grant sent Gen. William T. Sherman and two brigades after Beauregard, but they were stopped at Fallen Timbers by the Confederates under Col.

Nathan Forrest. Another victory for Grant, the successful stand at Shiloh served to bottle up the Confederates for several months.

**51.** The center of the Union position at Shiloh on April 6. The press reported that the unit illustrated here lost 48 horses and 30 men killed and wounded in fifteen minutes.

**52.** Shiloh on the second day, April 7, 1862, the recapture of artillery by the First Ohio and other regiments, under General Rousseau. The soldiers on the right are pictured in an impossibly regular formation, often seen in newspaper illustrations from the period, not all of which were drawn from first-hand observation. This was especially true of battles at remote places like Shiloh, where not many noncombatants were present. The paraphernalia of battle is always the same, however—the abandoned drums, the broken wagon wheels, the saddle-bags and cannonballs, fallen horses, tattered flags, men carried off on stretchers, soldiers loading and reloading, the lookout on the roof, the officers' raised swords, and the sight of those still living fighting beside the bodies of the dead. Estimated casualties at Shiloh—over 13,000 dead and wounded on the Union side, and over 10,000 on the Confederate side.

53

54

55

**53.** The week of the first anniversary of the attack on Fort Sumter saw a large Union naval force embarking on a mission to capture the south's largest city, New Orleans, and solidify control of the Mississippi River. Illustrated here is the first day's bombardment of Forts Jackson and St. Philip on the Mississippi, approximately seventy miles below New Orleans. These forts were the only obstacles to the invading Union expedition. Basing his operations on Ship Island, Mississippi, Flag Officer David G. Farragut assembled twenty-four ships of his West Gulf Blockading Squadron. His squadron was joined by nineteen mortar schooners under Comdr. David D. Porter. On April 16 the mortar schooners began the bombardment of Fort Jackson (illustrated here), which continued for several days. While the fort remained viable in Confederate hands, their guns were unable to inflict much damage on Farragut's fleet, and some of Farragut's ships opened a way through the obstructed river on the night of the 22nd. Finally, on the 24th, Farragut's main fleet passed the two forts and headed for New Orleans, where, though they incurred some damage and casual-

ties, Farragut reached his objective and accepted the city's surrender on April 28. On May 1, Union troops under Maj. Gen. Benjamin Franklin Butler began landing and occupying the city. With the fall of New Orleans, the garrisons of the two Confederate forts were swiftly cut off and surrounded, and they soon surrendered. The capture of the Confederacy's largest city and vital port was an event of major significance.

**54.** A scene from the battle for New Orleans, a blast from one of the Confederate guns at Fort Jackson hitting the Union gunboat *Iroquois* on April 24, killing 8 and wounding 7 members of a Dahlgren gun crew.

**55.** The Union gunboat *Hartford* on fire in the Mississippi during the Union effort to reach New Orleans in April 1862. Despite the attack by a Confederate ram, the *Manassas*, and a fire raft, a burning, floating projectile designed to set opposing ships on fire, the *Hartford* stayed afloat and made it past Forts Jackson and St. Philip.

56

56. A small segment of McClellan's army moving through the Virginia woods during the Peninsular Campaign of 1862. This illustration gives a good idea of the scale of this kind of operation, which involved tens of thousands of soldiers with their wagons and artillery, forcing their way overland often through, around, and over dirt roads turned into mud swamps, fallen trees, overflowing creeks, and impassable woods. Progress was slow and cumbersome. The Peninsular Campaign of 1862 was a major effort to take Richmond. McClellan's troops made some progress up the Virginia peninsula, occupying Yorktown on May 4, but the campaign's first phase ended with the indecisive battle at Seven Pines on May 31 and June 1. A short period of relative inactivity followed, during which overall command of the Confederate Army of Northern Virginia passed from Joseph E. Johnston, badly wounded at Seven Pines, to Robert E. Lee. Following a series of battles in late June, the Seven Days Battles, it was clear that Richmond wasn't going to be taken in 1862 and McClellan began to withdraw his troops back toward Washington.

57. An episode of the Peninsular Campaign of 1862, General Ambrose Burnside climbing the rigging of his ship off Cape Hatteras to give orders to his troops. As a diversion from the planned overland campaign toward the Confederate capital at Richmond, McClellan had Burnside take his Ninth Corps by ship from Roanoke Island to attack Confederate positions on the coast of North Carolina. While McClellan's campaign eventually failed

to take Richmond, Burnside's expedition was a success. The expedition left Roanoke on March 11, 1862, and after several hours of heavy fighting on March 14, the Union troops under his command had captured nine forts and forty-one heavy guns, and had established a base on the North Carolina coast that would be maintained for the duration of the war.

58. A different aspect of army life in a massive operation such as the Peninsular Campaign of 1862. Here a large contingent of McClellan's troops are heading for work in the campaign against Richmond with rifles on their backs, but more prominent on this occasion are the shovels to be used for digging trenches.

Overleaf: 59. One of the greatest Civil War illustrations, Winslow Homer's "The War for the Union, 1862—A Bayonet Charge," published in Harper's Weekly at the time of the 1862 Peninsular Campaign. Harper's reported that Homer had spent some time with the Army of the Potomac and captured the energy, the intensity, and the danger of the life faced by the Civil War soldiers.

Pages 48–49: 60. "New from the War" by Winslow Homer, published by Harper's right after his "Bayonet Charge" of 1862, is a panorama of vignettes of soldiers and civilians sending and receiving news from the front, wherever it might be or wherever they might be, during the endless campaigns of 1862.

57

58

For the Fleet.

News for the Staff.

Our special Artist.

60

61

62

63

61. Skirmishing in the Virginia woods during the Peninsular Campaign of 1862.

62. Another scene of army life at the time of the Peninsular Campaign, out of sight, waiting for action.

63. A lively recruiting drive in Philadelphia for the Pennsylvania Bucktails in August 1862. This famous regiment, known for the deer tails worn with their headgear and for the rowdy enthusiasm with which they went into battle, fought all over Virginia with the Army of the Potomac in the campaigns of 1862 and suffered so many casualties that recruiting was necessary a year into the war.

64

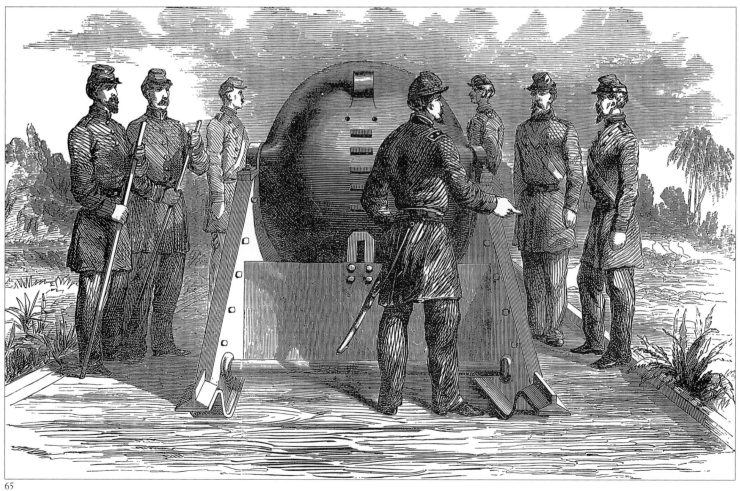

65

66

64. The heaviest weapon of the Civil War, the 17,000-pound, 13-inch shell mortar was used throughout the conflict, including many crucial campaigns during 1862.

65. Rear view of 13-inch mortar, illustrating also the usual complement of seven gunners needed to operate it at peak efficiency. The mortar was used for firing shells into camps or towns. It was also used for shelling fortifications on elevations, since cannons couldn't be used because of the height needed.

66. Thirteen-inch mortars in action during the bombardment of Fort Pulaski, April 10, 1862. Fort Pulaski, built by the army before the Civil War at the mouth of the Savannah River, was considered impregnable, but improvements in artillery changed that picture quickly. Following the bombardment of the fort on April 10–11, 1862, the Confederate commander, unable to halt the shelling and fearing the explosion of his magazine, surrendered to the Union forces outside.

*Overleaf:* 67. There is no question that the major American illustrated newspapers of the Civil War period, *Harper's Weekly* and *Frank Leslie's*, were highly partisan. They were published in the North, they were mostly read in the North, and they were devoted to the Union cause. They certainly included stories of skill in combat, chivalry, and courage by Confederate soldiers, sailors, and politicians, but their thrust was always pro-Union. As the war wore on, part of their efforts were devoted—sometimes openly, sometimes less openly—to propaganda. This illustration by the great Thomas Nast from *Harper's Weekly* in the fall of 1862 is a fascinating historical and political document. Nast, taking time off early in his career from local New York politics, drew this illustration entitled "A Rebel Guerrilla Raid in a Western Town," which *Harper's* published along with many lurid accounts of the depredations of guerrilla raiders and famous leaders such as William Quantrill (and unknown ones as well) on the ordinary citizens of the remote Western towns on which they preyed. Everything is here—wild drinking, casual shooting, killing helpless animals, raiding property, scaring the children, intimidating the local citizenry, lynching the odd Yankee sympathizer, abducting women, burning down the church—all of which taking place before the eyes of some so jaded or drunk that they are only mildly interested or aren't paying attention at all. The element of harsh reality behind this portrayal no doubt made it all the more effective.

*1862: Fort Henry to Fredericksburg* | 53

67

PLANTER'S HOTEL.

68. *Harper's* most distinguished military correspondent, A. R. Waud, drew this illustration from first-hand observation of the First Maryland Battery in the thick of the action at Antietam on September 17, 1862.

**69.** Antietam was a day of attacks and counterattacks across a wide area. At a crucial juncture, Burnside's troops scored heavily against the Confederate right flank. Illustrated here is the successful bayonet charge of a Union Zouave Regiment against a Confederate battery. Not one of the six Confederate artillery pieces is actually being fired as the action unfolds.

70

71

72

73

70–72. Scenes of the devastating aftermath of Antietam, a series of wood engravings based on photographs by the famous Civil War photographer, Mathew Brady of Washington, who toured the battlefield and recorded these images right after the battle. McClellan confronted Robert E. Lee's Army of Northern Virginia at Sharpsburg, Maryland, near Antietam Creek, on September 16, 1862. The following day was a long series of thrusts and counterthrusts with neither side able to consolidate a victory. Outnumbered, Lee committed his entire army while McClellan kept part of his in reserve, possibly enabling the Confederates to fight to a draw by doing so. At night the armies regrouped and organized their positions. Skirmishing followed throughout the next day, but Lee finally withdrew toward Virginia and McClellan let him go. While generally considered inconclusive, the South's failure to defeat McClellan's superior numbers and the enormous casualties taken (2,108 Union soldiers killed, 9,549 wounded; 2,700 Confederate soldiers killed, 9,029 wounded) weighed enormously on the Confederate war effort. It has often been claimed that the inconclusive ending at Antietam convinced the British and French governments to hold off on according the Confederacy their previously contemplated official recognition, which would have been a huge blow to the Union and Lincoln's administration. In the aftermath of the battle, Lincoln issued the preliminary Emancipation Proclamation on September 22, 1862, announcing that slaves in all areas of the country in rebellion against the Union would be free as far as the federal government was concerned as of January 1, 1863. These illustrations record the dead on the battlefield, and a very pastoral vision of the stone bridge over Antietam Creek, across which, at a crucial juncture, some of Burnside's troops fought their way, taking many casualties.

73. This illustration by *Harper's* artist Thomas Nast shows Lee's army retreating back across the Potomac under cover of night following Antietam. Lee's foray into Maryland led to the single bloodiest day in American military history, but eventually his Army of Northern Virginia had to withdraw back to Virginia and the Shenandoah Valley without the victory they wanted and needed. Almost a year would pass before Lee would lead his men to another fateful confrontation north of Virginia, this time at Gettysburg.

74.

**74.** Soldiers of Confederate General Braxton Bragg's army attacking the Union position at Munfordville, Kentucky, an important railroad connection on the line of the Louisville and Nashville Railroad on September 14, 1862. After a few days of fighting, Confederate officers convinced the commander of the Union garrison there to surrender to superior numbers and this important transportation center and bridge across the Green River came under the control of the Confederacy.

**75.** At Lincoln's order, the veteran Union General A. E. Burnside took command of the Army of the Potomac in early November 1862. Here Burnside issues orders on horseback to his staff immediately after taking over this command. Burnside acted quickly, occupying positions around Falmouth and Fredericksburg, in the crucial Virginia country between Washington and Richmond, but his ill-fated assault on the Confederates' position at Fredericksburg in the following month ended the year with a major debacle for the Union Army and his command.

**76.** Burnside's headquarters at Weaverville during the Fredericksburg campaign.

75

Gen! Burnside's headquarters at Weaverville.

76

77. A wagon train supporting Burnside's army near Falmouth, Virginia, in the days leading up to the futile assault on the Confederates' position at Fredericksburg on December 11–15, 1862. Reacting to Burnside's position near Falmouth, Lee entrenched his forces on the hills behind Fredericksburg. On December 11, the Union Army engineers, under fire, successfully laid a pontoon bridge across the Rappahannock River, which Burnside's forces crossed on the 12th. Between the 13th and the 15th, Burnside's forces mounted a series of futile assaults against the Confederate position, and took enormous casualties as a result, over 13,000 dead and wounded to less than a third of that total for Lee's troops. Another ineffective campaign in January 1863 led to Burnside's replacement by Maj. Gen. Joseph Hooker.

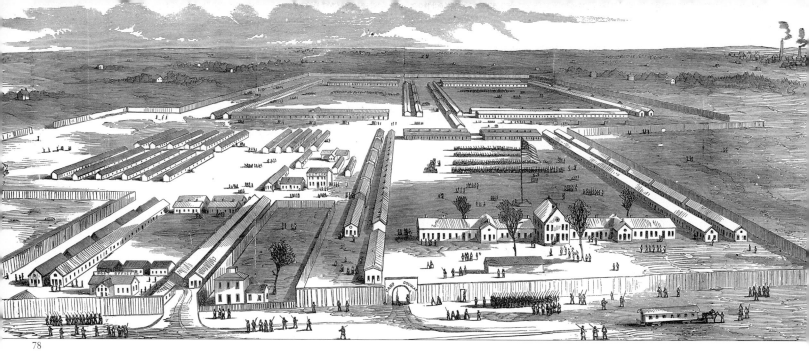

78

**78.** Even though the action never reached Chicago, the city was still affected by the events of the Civil War far to its south. This is a view of Camp Douglas in 1862 at the location of present-day 31st Street and Cottage Grove Avenue. Built as a Union training base, Camp Douglas housed approximately 26,000 Confederate prisoners between 1862 and 1865, beginning with 8,000 captured at Fort Donelson in Tennessee in February 1862. Living in temporary wooden barracks under harsh conditions similar to those in other Civil War prison camps, about 4,000 Confederate prisoners died there and were buried in unmarked pauper's graves in the City Cemetery of Chicago in part of what is now Lincoln Park. These remains were later moved several miles to Oak Woods Cemetery.

**79.** A peaceful and placid encampment of Union troops on New York's Long Island in December 1862, preparing the next wave of soldiers heading south for the war.

79

# 1863
## *Chancellorsville to Chattanooga*

JANUARY 1, 1863, was the effective date of the Emancipation Proclamation, which declared that all slaves in states then in rebellion against the Union were free men in the eyes of the federal government. In the first year of his presidency, Lincoln had resisted issuing such a Proclamation in an attempt to maintain the loyalty of slave-holding border states, but as the Civil War progressed, political opinion in the North moved increasingly toward abolition, and the Emancipation Proclamation, issued the previous fall but with the effective date of January 1, 1863, was the legal and formal recognition of the inevitable. In addition to freeing the slaves, following the Proclamation, black soldiers could be enlisted in the Union Army. Organizationally, January 1863 saw Joseph Hooker replace Ambrose Burnside as commander of the Army of the Potomac and Grant took command of the Army of the West with orders to take the crucial Confederate stronghold of Vicksburg, Mississippi. In March 1863, the Union, realizing it was facing recruiting problems, declared all men between the ages of 20 and 45 subject to conscription. Service could be avoided by either finding a substitute or paying a $300 fee, which provoked riots in working-class areas later that summer in New York City and in other cities as well. Reaction in the South to the Confederacy's similar conscription act was more or less the same.

In the first week of May, Lee's smaller army scored a major victory over Hooker at Chancellorsville in Virginia, the result of Lee's brilliant tactics. Hooker was forced to withdraw his troops back across the Rappahannock River, but on May 10, the Confederacy suffered a major blow when Stonewall Jackson, inadvertently wounded at Chancellorsville by his own soldiers, died of pneumonia following the amputation of his arm. Huge casualty numbers were by then becoming routine. Almost 200,000 troops opposed each other at Chancellorsville (130,000 on the Union side), and the battle left 30,000 of them dead and wounded. In the Southern theater, Grant mounted a successful campaign against the fortified city of Vicksburg.

Grant's siege of Vicksburg began on May 22, and six weeks later, the Confederate General John Pemberton surrendered the city and his 30,000 troops. With the capture of Port Hudson shortly thereafter, the entire Mississippi River was under Union control, and the Confederacy would remain divided by the river.

Following up his success against Hooker at Chancellorsville, Lee decided to take the offensive to the North. On June 13, he scored a victory at Winchester, Virginia, and continued north to Pennsylvania with his 75,000-man army. Hooker, still focusing on the Confederate capital of Richmond, was then forced to abandon those plans and follow Lee north. In late June, Hooker resigned and was replaced by George Meade as commander of the Army of the Potomac, that Army's fifth commander in less than a year. Lee and Meade met at Gettysburg in Pennsylvania in the first days of July. Meade had greater numbers and stronger defensive positions; his troops won the furious battle at Gettysburg but failed to pursue Lee back to Virginia. Gettysburg marked the Civil War's turning point. It was the farthest north that Lee's army would advance, and defeat there also marked the end of any chance of the Confederacy's being recognized by foreign governments. A few months after the battle, on November 19, 1863, Lincoln delivered the Gettysburg Address at a ceremony designating a portion of the battlefield as a national cemetery.

After Gettysburg, the next major battle was at Chickamauga Creek on the Tennessee-Georgia border. The Confederates controlled the battlefield after the fighting of September 19–20 and the Union Army of the Cumberland under Gen. William S. Rosecrans retreated to the vital railroad center of Chattanooga, where they faced a siege by the Confederates. Grant won a brilliant victory there in November over the Confederate troops that seemed to be in control of the surrounding mountains. Grant broke the Confederate siege and paved the way for Sherman's Atlanta campaign the following year.

**80.** Union troops occupying Fort Hindman, Arkansas, on January 11, 1863. The Confederate command surrendered Fort Hindman following a combined Union land and naval assault that had gone on for two days. The Union attack on Fort Hindman at Arkansas Post on the Mississippi River was part of the overall campaign against the Confederate stronghold at Vicksburg. The capture of Fort Hindman didn't materially contribute to the Union victory the following July, but it did remove another obstacle to Union shipping on the Mississippi.

81

**81.** Explosion aboard the U.S.S. *Westfield* in Galveston Bay on January 1, 1863. As 1862 came to an end, the Texas port city of Galveston was in Union hands and its recapture was a major priority of the Confederate commander in Texas, Maj. Gen. John B. Magruder. The Confederates launched a coordinated land and sea attack on the Union forces at Galveston on New Year's Day. The attack was successful, and when the Confederates boarded the Union ship *Harriet Lane*, the *Westfield*, which was the flagship of Union Cdr. W. B. Renshaw, ran aground trying to come to her assistance. The Union sailors on the *Westfield* were abandoning their ship, as illustrated here, when she blew up prematurely, causing many deaths and injuries. Galveston fell back into the control of the Confederacy, but the Union blockade continued to limit traffic into and out of the harbor there.

**82.** Elements of the Banks Expedition landing at Baton Rouge, Louisiana, March 1863.

**83.** The Union bombardment of Fort Sumter early in April 1863. The fort was still of no military significance to the Union effort, but its symbolic value made it a target for a major effort. The effort failed. The bombardment didn't accomplish much and the infantry units massed for the operation were not landed. Several Union ironclads took part; one of them, the *Keokuck*, was hit more than 90 times by Confederate return fire and sank the following day. Later in the summer, another Union expedition arrived off Charleston to resume the campaign. Morris Island, off the coast south of Charleston, was taken after sixty days of shelling from Union ships, but this was an event of no major significance and the city of Charleston itself remained unoccupied for the duration of the war.

82

83

84

85

**84–85.** Army life in 1863, two scenes of Union soldiers going about their daily business at the time of Chancellorsville. **84:** A Union courier sits on his horse having a pipe while in the distance another mounted courier heads toward him with dispatches to be delivered to the next station along the line. **85:** An officer stopped by a guard outside a Union camp at night.

**86.** Union soldiers building a pontoon bridge across the Rappahannock River for the use of Gen. John Sedgwick's diversionary force, which would use it to cross the river below the Confederate position at Fredericksburg before the battle of Chancellorsville. Pontoon bridges of the kind illustrated here were used many times during the Civil War. They could be built relatively quickly to move soldiers, wagons, artillery, and other supplies across a river and into position for a battle, and could be dismantled just as quickly afterward. The pontoons could then be hauled to the next site on wagons.

In the aftermath of the Union debacle at Fredericksburg in December 1862, Lee's and Hooker's troops spent the winter facing each other across the Rappahannock River. In April the never-ending campaign for Virginia began again. On the 27th, Hooker dispatched cavalry units to prevent Lee from retreating away from Fredericksburg. Two days later, Hooker followed this move up by sending a small diversionary force across the Rappahannock below Fredericksburg, on the bridge constructed for this purpose shown in the illustration here, while his main force crossed the river upstream. On the first of May, Hooker's main force was near Chancellorsville, a crossroads west of Fredericksburg in a heavily wooded area known as the Wilderness. In the dense woods, Union superiority in artillery wasn't as great an asset as it was on an open battlefield and the Union force's superior numbers made less of a difference than usual. Without needed cavalry, Hooker lacked good intelligence about Lee's movements and on May 2, Confederate units under Stonewall Jackson routed the Union right flank. Hooker withdrew at that point and Lee forced the Union army in Virginia to retreat north of the Rappahannock during the next few days. Casualties were massive on both sides. While the battle was a Confederate victory that took some pressure off Richmond and Lee's army in Virginia, the loss of Jackson was devastating. Ironically, Lee's greatest victory as a general carried with it the seeds of his ultimate failure. The success of his indomitable fighting men and his brilliant tactics at Chancellorsville gave Lee the confidence to point his army north toward Pennsylvania and the debacle that awaited it at Gettysburg.

87

87. A stampede during the action at Chancellorsville.

88. The Army of the Potomac on the march.

89. Confederate prisoners captured at Chancellorsville.

*Overleaf:* 90. Ferocious fighting during Grant's attack on the fortified Confederate position at Vicksburg, Mississippi, on May 22, 1863. The Confederate position consisted of a chain of forts connected by trenches that stretched for several miles. When this direct assault failed, the six-week siege of the Confederate position began. The siege ended with the Confederate General John Pemberton's surrender in early July, just as the fighting at Gettysburg was also coming to an end.

*Pages 74–75:* 91. Another view of the action at Vicksburg during the attack on May 22, 1863, at another part of the Union position looking toward the Confederate lines in the distance. The action shown here seems almost like a lull in the battle with a few infantrymen and artillery units taking shots across the intervening space between the lines while others smoked and rested in the covered trenches.

88

89

94

**92.** The siege of Vicksburg, Gen. Sherman's position on the extreme right of the Union lines during the siege. Note the soldier relaxing with a copy of *Harper's Weekly*.

**93.** An unusual view of life in the trenches besieging Vicksburg, makeshift quarters set up by Union soldiers in the deep ravines around the Confederate position. These particular quarters housed a part of Union Gen. John Macpherson's Seventeenth Army Corps.

**94.** Union Gen. James B. McPherson, holding the compass, and two of his engineers during the siege of Vicksburg. McPherson was credited for his engineering skill in creating the Union trenches and other installations that proved to be so valuable during the long siege at Vicksburg.

Vicksburg, Mississippi, was a Confederate stronghold on the east bank of the Mississippi River halfway between Memphis, Tennessee, and New Orleans. Following the Confederacy's losses in 1862 of Fort Henry, Fort Donelson, and Memphis in Tennessee, combined with the fall of New Orleans the same year, Vicksburg was the last remaining Confederate stronghold on the Mississippi. The capture of Vicksburg by Grant's army in the early summer of 1863 divided the eastern and western states of the Confederacy by giving the Union total control of the Mississippi, and propelled Grant to the front rank of Union generals.

Vicksburg was a good site for a defensive position, on bluffs above the Mississippi and protected on the north by swampy bayous. Confederate batteries on the bluffs could overpower any assault by boat from the river, and an attempt to take Vicksburg by Union ironclads failed in May 1862. With other options seeming equally unfeasible, Grant devised a plan to attack the Confederate position from the high ground east of Vicksburg behind Confederate lines. He took 40,000 Union soldiers across to the west bank of the Mississippi, moved south and recrossed the river at Bruinsburg, thirty miles below Vicksburg, recrossing the river on a flotilla of Union ships commanded by Admiral David D. Porter that had successfully run past the Confederate batteries at Vicksburg. Once on the east side of the Mississippi, Grant moved north, leaving his supply lines behind and living off the land.

Grant made progress toward Vicksburg, taking Port Gibson on May 2 and Grand Gulf the following day. Confederate units led by Gen. Joseph E. Johnston and the overall commander at Vicksburg, John C. Pemberton, failed to link up with each other to confront Grant, and Pemberton retreated to Vicksburg. By May 18, Grant had reached the rear of the Confederate position at Vicksburg with Pemberton secure there but isolated. The Union assaults pictured on the previous two spreads failed to dislodge the Confederate army in Vicksburg and the long siege began. Grant's masterful maneuvering had left the Union forces in control of all the approaches to the city, and as June wore on, Pemberton's troops began to run out of ammunition and both his soldiers and the few thousand civilians who remained there found themselves facing actual starvation. With no way to receive supplies or reinforcements, and with his men staying alive by eating their horses, their mules, and eventually even their dogs because there was nothing else to eat, Pemberton surrendered on July 4, 1863, the day after the last battle at Gettysburg. As he had done the year before at Fort Donelson, Grant had, for the second time in the war, captured an entire Confederate army. Gettysburg and Vicksburg combined to make the summer of 1863 the turning point of the Civil War.

95

96

97

**95.** Union sharpshooters during the siege with the city of Vicksburg and the Mississippi River in the distance.

**96.** During the siege of Vicksburg, Pemberton's forces were penned up in the city between Grant's army to the east and Admiral David Porter's fleet of Union gunboats on the Mississippi. This sketch by *Harper's* staff artist Theodore R. Davis shows ships from Porter's fleet arriving at the Vicksburg levee on July 4, 1863, just after Pemberton's surrender. Davis sent the sketch to *Harper's* with the comment that he thought he had captured the moment well enough but for one element—he just couldn't portray the intense Mississippi summer heat.

**97.** Union assault with hand grenades on a part of the Confederate position during the siege of Vicksburg. The hand grenades in use then were primitive. There were many accounts of grenades that fired too soon, grenades that didn't fire at all, and grenades that were so late in firing that they were picked up and thrown back against the soldiers who had first launched them.

Pemberton's surrender at Vicksburg followed standard Civil War protocol. Once the decision to surrender had been made, two senior Confederate officers approached the Union lines under a flag of truce, were blindfolded, and taken to meet with a member of Grant's staff who passed along their message to Grant. Grant sent back the message that he would meet with Pemberton at an appointed time and place. At their meeting, the two generals talked for two hours and parted, according to observers, with a friendly handshake. Some time later the Confederate units at Vicksburg marched out of their positions and stacked up their weapons and flags while Grant and his senior staff rode into the city they had just captured. Vicksburg had cost the South not only Pemberton's army, but the Mississippi as well. For the remainder of the war it would be a Union river, under their enemy's control, dividing the Confederacy east and west.

98

99

100.

**98.** Union soldiers on the Gettysburg hill known as Little Round Top on July 2, 1863, the middle day of the three-day battle.

**99.** Union artillery at Gettysburg, also on July 2.

**100.** Union officers surveying the action at Gettysburg.

The climactic battle of the Civil War, often described as the greatest battle ever fought in the Western Hemisphere, was fought at Gettysburg, Pennsylvania, in rolling farmland fields and hills thirty-five miles southwest of Harrisburg, on July 1–3, 1863. After Gettysburg, any hopes the South might still have had for a definitive military victory were inestimably diminished, though final victory for the North was still almost two full years away. In addition, any hopes they might still have had for foreign intervention on their behalf, which many were able to recall had been crucial to American success in the Revolutionary War, were clearly gone forever.

After his victory over Hooker at Chancellorsville, Lee, confident in his soldiers, his officers, and his own ability as a tactician, ordered his 75,000-man army north into Pennsylvania. The forward Confederate troops under Gen. R. S. Ewell focused on the little country crossroads of Gettysburg. Union Gen. John Buford, commanding the advance cavalry of the Army of the Potomac, which was now under a new overall commander, Gen. George S. Meade, recognized the importance of Gettysburg as a road center, and was determined to hold it until reinforcements could reach him there. They soon did, while some of Lee's cavalry units were atypically late in linking up with his main army. By the first of July, the stage was set.

The fighting on the first day was inconclusive, and the second day saw attacks and counterattacks by both sides over the famous Gettysburg landmarks, Little Round Top, Cemetery Hill, Devil's Den, the Wheatfield, and the Peach Orchard. Lee ordered a final attack on July 3, sending Maj. Gen. George E. Pickett on his famous charge against the Union center. Fifteen thousand Confederate infantrymen threw everything they had at the Union lines, taking tremendous losses as they did. They broke through the Union position but were unable to hold their advantage. Under constant attack from all sides, pounded by artillery, with no reinforcements in sight, the Confederate forces had to retreat, leaving hundreds of prisoners behind. On the 4th of July, Lee gave up waiting for an attack that never came and began the long retreat into Virginia under the cover of a heavy rain, an endless wagon train carrying the wounded stretching for miles and miles behind the main body of his army. Lee accepted responsibility for the disaster, riding out himself to tell the remnants of Pickett's offensive that the disaster had been his fault, and later offering his resignation to Jefferson Davis. Pickett never forgave Lee. "That old man had my division slaughtered," he still said years later, but Davis declined to accept Lee's resignation.

The Union side wasn't much happier. Like many commanders of major land engagements in the Civil War, Meade was either unable or too cautious to follow up, and Lee was able to take his wounded army back to Virginia. However, the Union troops had been left in possession of the field, Lee's army had been turned back, and the invasion of Pennsylvania had been stopped and would never come again, all of this at enormous cost on both sides. After the three days of Gettysburg, 23,000 of the 88,000 Union troops there were dead or wounded, as were 20,000 of the 75,000 Lee had brought north to Pennsylvania. Lincoln was furious. "He [Lee] was within your easy grasp," he wrote to Meade, "and to have closed upon him would, in connection with our other late successes (*i.e.* the Confederate surrender at Vicksburg), have ended the war. As it is, the war will be prolonged indefinitely."

**101.** The Confederate attack on the Union position at Cemetery Hill, at Gettysburg, on July 2, 1863. The stone structure at the top left was the entrance to the cemetery for which the hill was named. The attack was repelled with tremendous casualties on both sides.

**102.** The Gettysburg countryside, rolling hills and huge open spaces; in peacetime an idyllic space, in wartime perfectly designed for two huge armies to inflict enormous damage on each other. Below this, another view of the action at Cemetery Hill, this time from inside the Union position near the entrance to the cemetery, looking down the hill toward the attacking Confederate troops.

*Overleaf:* **103.** Photographs taken at the scene that still exist show *Harper's* great battle artist, A. R. Waud, sitting on the side of a Gettysburg hill, sketchbook in hand, recording the chaos and destruction all around him. Among the many illustrations he sent back to New York from Gettysburg was this one of Union troops on the right engaging at close quarters the forces of Confederate General James Longstreet on the left, with Blue Ridge in the distance.

Emmittsburg, Md. Gen. Meade's Army pursuing Gen. Lee.

104

**104–107.** Four scenes of the New York City Draft Riots of July 1863: Rioters and military units clashing on the city's streets, the police battling rioters outside the *Tribune* offices, the lynching of a black man, and an illustration of the mob burning the "Colored Orphan Asylum" at Fifth Avenue and 46th Street. When the drawing of names for conscription into the Union Army began in New York City on July 11, 1863, discontent with the inequities of the new conscription system, combined with longer-standing racial and political attitudes, resulted in four days of anti-black violence on the city's streets. When the annual income of common laborers in northern cities was less than $500 a year, the mobs erupted in part over the policy that allowed anyone who could pay a $300 fee, or provide a willing substitute, to evade the draft. In New York City, and in other northern cities where antidraft violence also erupted at this time, antidraft agitation on the part of Irish and other white immigrant groups was closely allied to feelings of racial antagonism against recently emancipated slaves. Immigrant laborers in New York and elsewhere feared losing jobs to former slaves freed on the effective date of the Emancipation Proclamation, January 1, 1863, just six months earlier.

105

The antidraft violence was fueled by scurrilous propaganda spread by Democratic opponents of Lincoln and what they called "his" war. Why should poor white men, they argued, have to serve in a Union army that was fighting for the rights of former slaves to come north and take their jobs? In New York City and elsewhere, blacks and others were attacked on the streets and in their businesses while draft headquarters and other buildings were also attacked. Property damage was estimated at $1.5 million, a very substantial sum at that time. Over a hundred people were killed. Finally, after four days of violence, New York City police, combined with exhausted soldiers from the Seventh New York Regiment—recalled to help from Gettysburg, where the greatest battle of the war had ended just days before—were able to restore order. With the violence under control, the drawing of names for conscription proceeded without incident in August 1863, but even so, the nation's first experiment with conscription was heavily burdened with abuses. Draft quotas were established by Congressional district; some districts filled their quotas without needing the draft, and some did not. Many enterprising individuals found they could take a fee for substituting for the draft from one wealthy individual, then desert, head for another district, and do the same thing over again. On the other side of the ledger, some paid the $300 "commutation fee" to evade one draft call, then found themselves called again a short time later when a new quota was established.

106

107

108–109. *Violence against civilians wasn't limited to northern cities dealing with conscription in the summer of 1863. On August 21, 1863, William C. Quantrill led his band of a few hundred guerrillas, loosely allied with the Confederate army, to sack the free state stronghold of Lawrence, Kansas. At least 150 men, women, and children were shot or burned to death. Quantrill's raiders carried out other attacks in the remaining years of the war before Quantrill was* himself mortally wounded in Kentucky in 1865. No one from *Harper's* was actually in Lawrence when the attack occurred, but the scene was imaginatively recreated from descriptions in the ensuing weeks, including this view (109) of the rubble of buildings that had been burned down. The attacks themselves had been real enough and the "reenactments" in *Harper's* and other Northern papers served as anti-Confederate propaganda as the war dragged on.

110

**110.** Action resumed in Virginia in the weeks after Gettysburg. Here, at Culpeper on September 14, 1863, a Union cavalry brigade commanded by the very young Gen. George Armstrong Custer captured three Confederate artillery pieces.

**111.** In camp, 1863.

**112.** A less idyllic scene, the never-ending task of hauling artillery over the mountains through the rain and the mud. No one knows exactly how many horses served in the Civil War, but it was a staggering number.

*Overleaf:* **113.** The Battle of Chickamauga Creek, September 19–20, 1863. Chickamauga was a Confederate victory that failed to turn the tide. Two months later, ten miles away at Chattanooga, the results were reversed and the prologue to the war's final act was played out.

111

114

**114.** Union soldiers in the woods near Chattanooga as Confederate infantrymen using tree disguises approach on the right.

*Next page:* **115.** A lookout in the Union position at Chattanooga.

The city of Chattanooga, in southeastern Tennessee, on the Tennessee River near the Georgia border, was a strategic Confederate communication center and consequently a major objective of Union forces after Gettysburg. Following the battles of Chickamauga and Chattanooga in the fall of 1863, Union forces occupied Chattanooga, which then served as the base from which Gen. William Tecumseh Sherman launched his Atlanta campaign the following year.

After Gettysburg and Vicksburg in July, the focus shifted to the Confederate rail center of Chattanooga, Tennessee. At Chickamauga Creek on September 19–20, ten miles southeast of Chattanooga, the Union army under Gen. William S. Rosecrans was badly beaten in a fierce struggle involving much hand-to-hand combat and forced to retreat to Chattanooga by the Confederates under Braxton Bragg and James Longstreet. Union General George H. Thomas managed to hold the Union forces together during the aftermath of Chickamauga. Though a Confederate victory, Chickamauga (debate still goes on over whether this is actually an Indian word for "River of Death" as some have claimed—the description would certainly be an apt one) brought heavy casualties to both sides and Bragg was unable to follow up his victory. The results were reversed at Chattanooga two months later.

With Rosecrans' troops besieged in Chattanooga, Grant took over the campaign on the Union side and managed to break the siege and go on the offensive. After Union victories at Lookout Mountain and Missionary Ridge, the Confederates were in retreat, forced back over the Georgia line. Chattanooga paved the way for Sherman's 1864 march to Atlanta and Savannah and was in this way as decisive as Gettysburg and Vicksburg.

116

**116.** Confederate sharpshooters under the indefatigable Longstreet, attacking a Union wagon train near Chattanooga.

**117.** Union forces storming Missionary Ridge, the decisive end of the Chattanooga campaign.

**118.** Captured Confederate artillery, the aftermath of Chattanooga.

*Overleaf:* **119.** An episode of the aftermath of Chattanooga, the attempt by Confederate forces under Longstreet to drive Burnside's units from Knoxville. On November 29, 1863, Longstreet attacked Fort Saunders and took heavy casualties when his advancing units came upon a wide, deep ditch, which they had not expected to find, surrounding the fort. The ditch could not be crossed, and the Confederate soldiers, easy targets as they tried, failed, and then had nowhere to go, simply fell into it, dead and wounded on top of one another. The disaster at Fort Saunders marked the end of the siege of Knoxville.

120. Army life in the middle of the Civil War, Winslow Homer's account of "Payday in the Army of the Potomac."

SENDING MONEY HOME

THE LETTER

# 1864
## The Wilderness to Savannah

A BREATHER BEFORE the final act, the armies of both sides rested in the occasional snow and more constant cold of Virginia during the winter following the campaigns of 1863. Cities of tents filled the clearings in the woods and visiting newspaper correspondents found the men passing the time repairing equipment, playing cards, telling tall tales, and healing from minor injuries. Meanwhile, officers in more elaborate quarters—a larger tent, or perhaps an old farm-house borrowed for the season—wrote letters, studied their maps, and thought about the enemy encamped across the river in another part of the country. Soldiers from both sides with rifles over their shoulders walked the lonely perimeters trying to stay warm, watching for signs of life, hoping a party of sharpshooting snipers from the other side wasn't following their every movement from the undergrowth. For everyone, Union and Confederate alike, it was a quiet but uneasy time forced on them by the weather and the need to regroup. Everyone knew that it wouldn't last.

On the strategic level, it seems easy to think now that the war was really over when the winter of 1863–64 turned into spring and the armies started to move again. Vicksburg, Gettysburg, and Chattanooga, the great Union victories of 1863, were now all in the past. It would not be long into the campaigns of 1864 before the pattern of the action of these months would emerge. The South might have the better generals, the more astute tacticians, and the indomitable fighting spirit of an army fighting for a cause in which they passionately believed, but even with all of this, they were up against a harsh reality that nothing in their power could change. They had fewer men, less money and equipment, and had been abandoned by potential foreign allies. They also had a home front that had incurred many devastating losses and had suffered the economic consequences of three long years of combat and naval blockade, such as hunger, dire shortages, and rampant inflation. If someone could have stepped back and taken a hard look at the situation in April 1864 with the armies now up and rolling, it could easily have seemed like a tunnel to a dead end. The South could, and did, fight on through 1864 and beyond, but by then, they couldn't win. It would take another year of fighting, tens of thousands more dead bodies, tens of thousands more wounded veterans, before that reality was truly faced.

In May and June 1864, the Wilderness, Spotsylvania, and Cold Harbor were the sites of Grant's progressive attempt to crush Lee's army in Virginia, and Lee's successful effort to keep his dwindling and hard-pressed army alive. Some of the battles were inconclusive. Some Lee won, but every time,

win or draw, he emerged with fewer men to fight the next time. Grant certainly didn't get what he wanted from the first campaigns of 1864. For the Confederacy, Richmond was saved—for now—at tremendous cost and by June the armies of both sides settled into the long siege of Petersburg. Grant had hoped to take Petersburg and then strike at Richmond from the South. It was a reasonable plan, and nothing else had worked out, but it also failed, at least for 1864. As the summer wore on, Grant pushed his lines further and further west from Petersburg. The Confederates countered with their lines, the long front became longer, but Richmond still didn't fall until the following year. In mid-summer, the South made its final attempt at Washington as Gen. Jubal Early pushed into Maryland, hoping to lessen pressure on Lee and attack the Union's capital, but five miles from Washington was as close as he got and by mid-July Early had been forced back to Virginia's Shenandoah Valley. Union Gen. Philip Sheridan took on Early in the Shenandoah in the later part of the summer of 1864 and by the fall Early's army was finished and the Shenandoah was both devastated and under Union control. The focus of the war then shifted to Atlanta and the South and the campaign there of Gen. William Tecumseh Sherman against the Army of the Tennessee.

The North suffered 100,000 casualties in the massive campaigns of 1864, and by the end of the summer, with the presidential election on the horizon, morale was low and war-weariness on the upswing. Democrats were campaigning on a platform calling for an armistice with the Confederacy. The war, they argued, had been a failure, a costly, devastating, Republican failure, and a negotiated peace with the South was the only way out. For Lincoln the political handwriting seemed to be on the wall in large letters. "I am going to be beaten and unless some great change takes place badly beaten," he wrote to a friend in August. All of this was swept away by Sherman's march to Atlanta, and the significance of the capture of Atlanta was far greater than just the substantial resources that were taken out of the Confederacy's hands as a result. A military victory on such a massive scale, so far from Washington, achieved for once without devastatingly high casualties on the Union side, made it seem as if the end, or at least the beginning of the end, might be at hand at last. When nothing happened in the remaining weeks before the election to counter Union gains, and Sheridan's success in the Shenandoah played a part in this but a smaller part than Atlanta, Lincoln swept to an easy victory in November.

121

**121.** Workshops of the Army of the Potomac in the winter of 1864, preparing for the campaigns of the spring and summer to come. The armies of the Civil War traveled on foot, on horseback, and by wagon and when the fighting stopped in the winter months, the wagons had to be repaired and the wheels put back on as illustrated here. The off-kilter sign nailed to the leafless tree in the center of this engraving calls this place the General Headquarters, with a self-deprecating soldier's humor.

**122.** Edwin Forbes' illustration of army blacksmiths at work. The blacksmith's four-wheeled wagon compactly carried everything he needed to do his essential work—a portable anvil, tongs, iron for the horseshoes, coal to burn, a cast-iron pan for the fire, and a bellows to keep it going.

122

**123.** A guard at winter quarters, Army of the Potomac, 1864.

*Next page:* **124.** The Presentation of Colors to the Twentieth United States Colored Infantry at the Union League Clubhouse on Union Square in New York City on March 5, 1864. The Twentieth Regiment traveled by steamer from Riker's Island to the foot of 21st Street on the East River and then marched to Union Square, where a huge crowd heard President King of Columbia College address the troops at the presentation of their colors. Comparable ceremonies marked the entrance of black units into the Union Army throughout the North after the Emancipation Proclamation. Two weeks after the presentation of the colors, the Twentieth was on duty in New Orleans. They served at several southern locations in the last two years of the war and were mustered out in October 1865.

125

**125.** An episode of the Red River Campaign of 1864, the capture of Fort DeRussy on the Red River in Louisiana on March 14, 1864, by Union troops commanded by Gen. Andrew Jackson Smith. Smith's force left Vicksburg on March 10 and reached Summerville, Louisiana, three days later. They took what some had believed to be the impregnable Fort DeRussy the following day with minimal casualties, opening the Red River to Alexandria.

**126.** A Union scout in Louisiana during the Red River Campaign of 1864. The Red River Campaign was a Union attempt to seize control of the cotton-growing states of Louisiana, Arkansas, and Texas.

Despite the capture of Fort DeRussy in March, the overall campaign failed. In early April, Union troops were defeated at Sabine Crossroads and forced to withdraw. There were no further significant Union operations in the area for the remainder of the war.

**127.** Part of Admiral David Porter's fleet on the Red River in March 1864. Porter provided nautical support for the Union's Red River Campaign. Despite the commitment of 20 warships, 40 transport ships, and 30,000 troops, the Red River Campaign of 1864 was a costly fiasco for the North, draining manpower that could have been better used elsewhere.

126

127

128

*Pages 108–109:* The three sketches on these pages were published in *The Illustrated London News* in April 1864, presenting drawings brought back to London by the paper's anonymous artist-correspondent who had spent time with the Confederate Army during the winter just past. The South had no illustrated papers to match *Harper's Weekly* and *Frank Leslie's*, and *The Illustrated London News'* Confederate bias provides a striking counterpoint to the pro-Union message always carried by the two New York papers.

**128.** The Winter Quarters of the Confederate Army on the Rapidan River in Virginia, the headquarters during the winter of 1863–64 of Robert E. Lee and his storied cavalry commander, J. E. B. Stuart. The *ILN's* correspondent may have added a small self-portrait here on the lower left. He reported a sense of time passing slowly in winter quarters, time spent waiting for spring, time spent with the consciousness that all around this peaceful scene, in almost any direction the eye could follow, were the bloody battlefields of the past three years and the graves of thousands of soldiers.

**129.** Cotton from a Southern ship, which had managed to evade the Union blockade, being unloaded for British merchant customers on the docks at Nassau in the West Indies in the late winter of 1864. Although England was a cotton-importing nation and many there had pro-Southern views for that reason, full diplomatic recognition for the Confederacy by the English government never became a reality and, after Gettysburg, was a dead issue.

**130.** The tent on the right in this engraving was the winter headquarters of Confederate General J. E. B. Stuart, who was killed in action at Yellow Tavern soon after the campaigns of 1864 began.

129

130

131

**131.** The Fort Pillow Massacre, April 12, 1864, a reminder to the Union, if one was needed, that the war was still going on beyond Virginia where Grant's resources were by then heavily concentrated on the never-ending campaign against Richmond. A Union garrison holding Fort Pillow, a Confederate-built earthen fort overlooking the Mississippi River about forty miles above Memphis, was overrun by a Confederate force commanded by Maj. Gen. Nathan Bedford Forrest. The 600-man Union garrison at Fort Pillow included 262 U.S. Colored Troops. When the Union commander, Gen. William F. Bradford, refused to surrender, Forrest drove the Union soldiers from the fort and into a deadly crossfire along the river. Only 62 of the U.S. Colored Troops survived the battle, and debate continues today as to whether the Confederates prolonged the fight for the purpose of killing black soldiers even after the fort had been taken. The Confederates immediately abandoned Fort Pillow after their victory, so the battle had little lasting military significance, but the claim that there had been a "Fort Pillow Massacre" was a rallying cry for the Union in the final year of the war.

*Next page:* **132.** The Confederate prison camp at Belle Isle, an island in the James River at Richmond, drawn for *The Illustrated London News* in 1864. The routine of exchanging prisoners broke down as the war continued, and by 1864 the numbers of prisoners being held by both sides were staggering. At Belle Isle, just outside the Confederate capital, the *ILN* reported that 7,000 Union soldiers and officers were being held, the officers in a former tobacco warehouse, the soldiers in the city of tents illustrated here. Although perhaps not as bad as the conditions at Andersonville and the worst Civil War prisons, Belle Isle was bad enough. As the prison population grew, there weren't enough tents to go around and exposure to the elements, poor rations, and little or no medical attention caused the death rate to rise. A considerable number of prisoners were willing to risk the perilous river currents and rifle fire from the guards, and a few did escape via the river. The city of Richmond is shown in the background with the Petersburg Bridge, and a Southern railroad train crossing it, on the right.

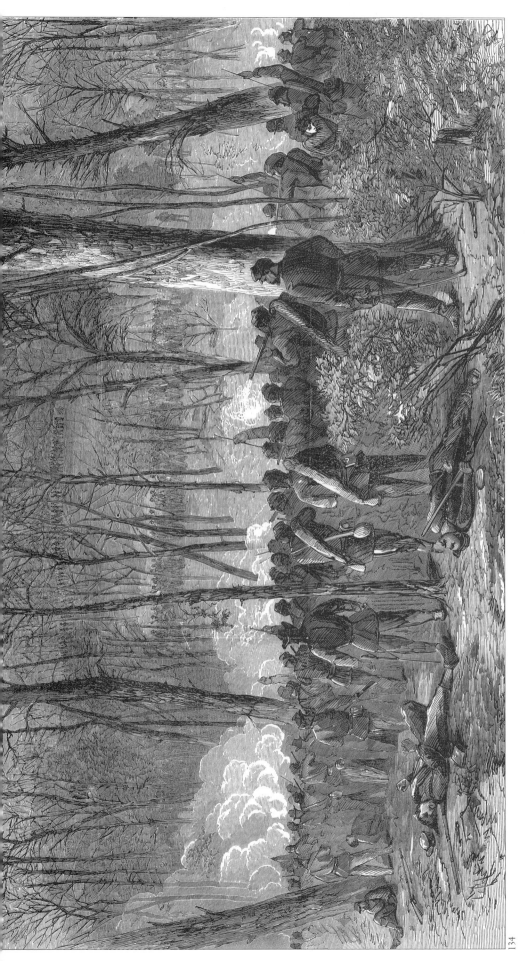

**133.** Before the Battle of the Wilderness, on the line of the Union Second Corps on May 6, 1864, soldiers waiting for the enemy: smoking, sleeping, playing cards, a few chopping down trees to provide wood for needed defenses and some sight lines through the trees. In the heavily wooded area of Virginia near Fredericksburg known as the Wilderness, the Union's numerical superiority in troops and artillery proved meaningless as organized, coordinated attacks were impossible to mount. The pipe-smoking figure at the lower right with the unusual headgear may represent the illustrated weekly's artist-correspondent. Getting involved in a battle in the forests of the Wilderness was a disastrous error for Grant. Fires ignited during the fighting turned the area into a rampant inferno.

Although some of the wounded were carried out by their fellow soldiers on makeshift slings made up from tents and blankets, many more were burned alive.

**134.** At the Wilderness, the shooting has started. Through the smoke and heavy trees, a glimpse of the enemy may be seen. As the Virginia campaign of 1864 began, Grant, recently promoted to the rank of lieutenant general and entrusted with overall commander of all Union armies, planned to engage Lee in Virginia until Lee's army was finished. Lee's Army of Northern Virginia and Joseph Johnston's Army of Tennessee were the only remaining major obstacles to an overall Union victory. The Wilderness was the first step in the campaign against Lee, but the three-day battle was not deci-

sive. Grant knew the Wilderness was not the ideal place for him to fight and had hoped to get through the area before Lee could move, but Lee was quick to respond and two days of heavy fighting in the woods was the result. Grant took heavier casualties than Lee at the Wilderness, but Lee had no replacements for his while Grant still had reserves to call on. What was ominous for the Confederacy as the battle ended on May 7 with Grant not retreating but moving east toward Spotsylvania Courthouse, in effect bringing his army out of the woods toward what might be a better place for them to fight, was the fact that the Union had been able to put over 100,000 troops in the field to Lee's 61,000, a disadvantage that would weigh on Lee's army as Grant's Overland Campaign of 1864 wore on.

135.

135. The Battle of Spotsylvania Courthouse, the second stop on the 1864 Virginia campaign, which would lead in the next six weeks through Spotsylvania, across the North Anna River, to Cold Harbor and finally to Petersburg. Spotsylvania Courthouse was a series of battles over a two-week period that included some of the fiercest fighting of the war. This is an illustration of Alsop's Farm, two miles north of Spotsylvania Courthouse, which gives an idea of the scale of the battles for Virginia in 1864. The Union almost delivered a body blow to Lee, coming close to dividing the Confederate Army in half in the dawn attack on the "Bloody Angle" on May 12–13, but Confederate counterattacks pushed back the threat in fighting that went on and on for hours. Finally, on May 21, Grant disengaged to continue his attack on Richmond elsewhere. The Union forces were twice the size of the Confederate forces at Spotsylvania— 100,000 to 50,000, respectively—and the Union side took 60 percent of the 30,000 casualties there. Despite heavy casualties, Spotsylvania was a victory for Lee in the long defense of Richmond, as he was able there to keep the larger Union Army at bay.

136. Horses and caissons during the Virginia campaign of 1864.

137. Edwin Forbes' sketch of former slaves caught up in the heart of warfare during the Virginia campaigns of 1864. They are seen here coming into a Union camp, their mismatched farm animals pulling an uncovered wagon. The wagon is carrying several generations of displaced slaves looking for some protection from the fighting all around them.

*Overleaf*: 138. The Battle of Yellow Tavern, May 11, 1864, a cavalry attack led by Union Gen. Philip Sheridan against the defenders of Richmond. The battle was a minor Union victory. There were only eight hundred casualties combined on both sides at Yellow Tavern, but one of them was devastating to the Confederacy. Gen. J. E. B. Stuart, Lee's brilliant cavalry commander, was mortally wounded in action at Yellow Tavern and died soon after the battle.

136

137

139

140

**139.** Union artillery firing at Cold Harbor. After Spotsylvania, Grant headed southeast to Cold Harbor, a strategic crossroads not far from Richmond, reaching there in early June 1864. At Cold Harbor, Grant attacked once more, and lost again, in what would prove to be Lee's last clear victory of the Civil War. The scale of the battle was huge. One hundred seventy thousand soldiers were involved on both sides, only 62,000 of them Confederates. By June 2, a front seven miles long reached from Bethesda Church to the Chickahominy River. A major Union attack on June 3 was a disaster; Grant wrote in his memoirs years later that it was the one attack in his life that he regretted ordering. In one twenty-minute period, the Union Army lost 7,000 men. Overall, the Union Army took 13,000 casualties during the two weeks of fighting at Cold Harbor, five times as many as the Confederates. However reluctantly, Grant came to the conclusion that Richmond wasn't going to be taken by any sort of direct assault just then, and headed his army south to Petersburg.

**140.** The infantry at Cold Harbor, June 1, 1864.

*1864: The Wilderness to Savannah* | 119

141

**141.** Stevens Battery, a Union artillery battery, at Cold Harbor.

**142.** General Barlow charging the Confederate position at Cold Harbor, June 1, 1864. Time after time at Cold Harbor, direct Union assaults on the Confederate positions forced Lee to take casualties he couldn't afford, but still failed to deliver the knockout Grant was hoping for. The blazing heat of the Virginia summer made it worse for everyone, especially for the hopelessly wounded men left on the battlefields.

*Overleaf*: **143.** Part realism, part reportage, part propaganda, Thomas Nast's "On To Richmond," published by *Harper's* during the Virginia campaigns of 1864. In a month of fighting in Virginia

in the summer of 1864, Grant had taken 50,000 casualties and had little to show for it. Lee's army had been pressed, stretched thin, and forced to maneuver, but had been up to the challenge, reeling from unrelenting combat with a bigger, more powerful enemy, but still viable. Lee had been able to avoid a huge defeat; Richmond was still safe. With nothing to gain by remaining at Cold Harbor, on the night of June 12, Grant began moving his army across the James River via a huge pontoon bridge, headed for the strategic rail center at Petersburg, twenty-five miles south of Richmond. His plan was that by taking Petersburg and the railroads centered there, he would force Lee to fight in the open where the Union's superiority in numbers and equipment would prove decisive. By the middle of June, Grant was outside Petersburg.

*1864: The Wilderness to Savannah* | 121

**144.** Union soldiers in the trenches at Petersburg. The man at left is playing cards and holding up a hat to see if he can draw enemy fire, while his fellow soldier to the right points out a bullet hole in his own hat. The long siege of Petersburg saw weeks of the casual exchange of fire from snipers and sharpshooters on both sides, as illustrated here.

**145.** A Union assault at Petersburg, soldiers from the Eighteenth Corps taking a portion of Beauregard's line. Not resting long after the devastation of Cold Harbor, elements of the Army of the Potomac attacked Beauregard's position at Petersburg on June 15, 1864. For two days, the action seemed to favor the Union attackers, but Beauregard consolidated his defenses and Lee quickly moved in reinforcements from the Army of Northern Virginia. By June 18, any chance that Petersburg might be captured quickly was gone and the long siege of the city was on.

146

**146.** A military signal station from the time of the Petersburg siege. After initial assaults on the Confederate position at Petersburg failed, Grant's army began digging in for an open-ended siege of the city. Grant's strategy was to continually extend his lines at Petersburg to the west, and ultimately this proved productive. As the front was continually being extended, Lee's already thin forces were stretched even farther. No doubt Grant was thinking that if the siege of Petersburg could produce the same result as the siege of Vicksburg a year earlier, it would be worth the effort. The siege of Petersburg was interrupted from time to time by dramatic events such as the "Battle of the Crater" on July 30, 1864. A unit of coal miners in the Union camp dug a tunnel from the Union position more than 500 feet long to a location under a Confederate artillery emplacement southeast of Petersburg. When the tunnel was completed, 8,000 pounds of gunpowder were placed at the end of it and detonated under the Confederate position. The explosion killed more than 250 Confederate soldiers and left a crater 170 feet long, 60 feet wide, and 30 feet deep, probably the largest single explosion produced in warfare in the history of the world before the atomic bombs dropped on Hiroshima and Nagasaki in 1945. The episode was dramatic but not significant; Union units advanced following the explosion but couldn't hold their gains and the Confederates retook the sector the same day. After the explosion Grant's officers concentrated on conventional siege tactics, building up their supplies and strengthening their forces in the trenches. On the other side of the lines, Lee's forces were continually hard-pressed as the summer and the siege wore on—hunger, disease, shortages of all kinds, desertions rising at an alarming rate—with no real way out in sight.

**147.** Union gunners from the Eighteenth Corps at Petersburg.

147

148

**148.** Union sharpshooters from the Eighteenth Corps in the trenches at Petersburg.

**149.** Firing a small mortar at Petersburg. Both of the engravings on this page were based on sketches by *Harper's* artist A. R. Waud.

149

150

**150.** A Confederate artillery battery on the south bank of the James River, part of the defense of Richmond in the summer of 1864. In the distance, some federal ironclads lie below the north bank, kept at bay by the Confederate guns in the foreground. In the river are obstructions placed there by the Union side to prevent Confederate ships from coming up the river to attack them. The net effect was a long standoff during which the tedium was sometimes overcome by each side taking long and generally ineffective shots at each other.

**151.** A Union soldier using a torch to signal in the summer of 1864, sending messages from a raised platform while another peers through his telescope for the reply.

**152.** The capture of the C.S.S. *Tennessee*. By the summer of 1864,

the focus of the conflict was on land, especially on the Virginia and Georgia battlefields, but the naval war also continued. A Union fleet of eighteen ships commanded by Rear Admiral David Farragut steamed into Mobile Bay on August 5, 1864, in an attempt to close the bay to blockade runners. They were confronted by Confederate Admiral Franklin Buchanan, whose flagship was the C.S.S. *Tennessee*, a formidable ironclad. One Union ironclad, the *Tecumseh*, struck a mine during the action and sank. After inflicting a lot of damage on several Union ships, the *Tennessee*, heavily damaged herself and moving slowly, was finally overpowered and captured by the Union ships *Monongahela* and *Lackawanna*, which also inflicted considerable damage on themselves while repeatedly ramming the *Tennessee*. Later that month, Union forces took Fort Morgan, virtually shutting down the port. The city of Mobile, however, was never captured.

151

152

**153.** Another scene from the later stages of Grant's Virginia campaign of 1864, the Fifth Corps attacking a Confederate redoubt at Peebles's Farm, September 30, 1864.

**154.** Cavalry charge at Winchester, Virginia, September 1864. In late September 1864, Winchester, in Frederick County, saw the most intense and significant action of Union Gen. Philip Sheridan's Shenandoah Campaign, as Sheridan's almost 40,000 troops met Gen. Jubal Early's 15,000 Confederates. Early was driven back and forced to retreat, taking almost 4,000 casualties, which by that time his forces couldn't afford.

155

**155.** Confederate troops snaking their way through Virginia's Shenandoah Valley in October 1864, in an attempt to reinforce the troops of Gen. Jubal Early. Early's forces had been successful in the first months of 1864 in the Shenandoah and had marched to within striking distance of Washington, D.C. before being halted at Fort Stevens in July. During the fighting there, Lincoln rode out to the front from Washington to watch the action, becoming the only American President ever under fire, albeit from a distance, in wartime. With no hope of taking Washington, Early headed back to the Shenandoah Valley. Back in the Shenandoah, a series of hard-fought losses to Sheridan's 40,000 Union troops would eliminate Early as a threat to the Union and would give the North control of the crucial Shenandoah for the rest of the war.

**156.** *Harper's* conception of Gen. Philip Sheridan's famous ride to the front to rally his troops during the Shenandoah campaign of 1864. Sheridan was at Winchester on October 19, 1864, having just returned to the Shenandoah Valley from a trip to Washington, when the fighting started at Cedar Creek, twenty miles away. Responding to reports that the fighting was not going well, Sheridan rode the twenty miles and rallied his forces to gain a substantial victory over Early, essentially bringing down the curtain on his successful Shenandoah campaign and providing, as Sherman did in Georgia, a victory that helped the reelection campaign of Abraham Lincoln. "Sheridan's Ride" became a larger than life episode, commemorated in an immensely popular and often reprinted poem by Thomas Buchanan Read.

**157.** Sheridan's army on the march in the Shenandoah. Once the Shenandoah campaign was successfully concluded, in the autumn of 1864, Sheridan took his army east to join forces with Grant in the ongoing campaign for Richmond. Though his army wasn't huge, it was a significant addition to the forces arrayed against Lee in the final months of the war, during a time when the Confederate forces were dwindling through attrition.

156

157

158

159

**158.** The area of Virginia around Richmond was one major theater in the decisive summer of 1864, the Shenandoah Valley was a second, and in the latter half of the year, the state of Georgia became the third. This engraving depicts Union Gen. William Tecumseh Sherman and his officers during the Atlanta campaign in July 1864. Grant and the others fought in Virginia all through the spring and summer of 1864, always keeping in mind the main prize, Richmond, the Confederate capital that seemed perpetually just beyond the Union's grasp. The Southern rail and munition center of Atlanta loomed as the last major objective, other than Richmond, that the Confederacy had to offer. Chattanooga was gone, had been for several months, and Sherman finally turned toward Atlanta. The brilliant Confederate General Joseph E. Johnston managed to delay and deter Sherman's way to Atlanta with a force half his opponent's size, less than 60,000 troops to Sherman's almost 120,000, but because of policy differences and internal politics, the Confederates replaced Johnston with Gen. John Bell Hood. Hood was a courageous soldier and inspiring leader who had already lost a leg and the use of one arm in combat, but he was not the equal of Johnston as a tactician and no match for Sherman and the superior resources of Sherman's army. After a few weeks of mounting casualties, Hood surrendered Atlanta on September 1, 1864, and Sherman's forces occupied the city the following day.

The victory at Atlanta was a great boost to Northern morale. Lincoln and the Union command had hoped for better results from the Virginia campaign, but hadn't received them. Atlanta changed the feeling in the North about the way the war was going, and thereby helped more than anything else did, to pave the way for the reelection of Lincoln in November 1864. It seems hard to believe that general war-weariness in the North at one point made reelection for Lincoln in 1864 seem unlikely, and a victory by his Democratic opponent, Gen. George B. McClellan, was widely forecast. Lincoln's popularity boomed after Sherman's victory in Atlanta, and Lincoln was reelected with a 55 percent to 45 percent majority in the popular vote, and with 212 of 233 electoral votes. One of the many "firsts" credited to the American Civil War is that it was the first war in which soldiers in the field paused in their fighting to vote in a general election.

**159.** The Battle of Kennesaw Mountain, June 27, 1864, a defeat for Sherman on his way to Atlanta. The Confederate army of Gen. Joseph E. Johnston was dug in at Kennesaw Mountain, northwest of Marietta, in a position to protect the Western & Atlantic Railroad, a crucial supply link to Atlanta. Sherman felt that the Confederate lines could be overrun, but after an artillery bombardment and some initial successes, Sherman was forced to withdraw with heavy casualties.

**160.** The destruction of the depots, public buildings, and manufacturers of Atlanta. The fighting for Atlanta was a long process, but the result was probably not in doubt after the Union troops approaching the city successfully defended themselves from a complex assault by Confederate Gen. John Bell Hood on July 22, 1864. Hood had planned a coordinated attack on Union Gen. James B. McPherson's Army of the Tennessee, but wasn't able to coordinate the efforts of every element, and after many attacks and counterattacks, the Union army held. At one point Sherman positioned twenty pieces of artillery on a hill near his headquarters to shell the Confederates. Union casualties were over three thousand, but the Confederates lost more than twice that many.

**161.** The citizens of Atlanta evacuating before Sherman's final assault.

162

162. Confederate prisoners taken during Sherman's Atlanta campaign.

163. Union soldiers foraging for food during the 1864 Atlanta campaign.

164. A halt on the march, Thomas Nast's conception of taking a break in a farmer's yard. At the time this illustration was published, Sherman had rested his troops in Atlanta and had then taken 62,000 of them on his march through Georgia to the sea. Living off the land, Sherman's troops marched three hundred miles, slicing a path sixty miles wide and destroying everything they saw—factories, railroads, bridges, and public buildings. Sherman captured Savannah on December 21 and sent Lincoln a famous telegram, offering him the city as a Christmas present.

163

164

# 1865
## *Fort Fisher to Appomattox*

EIGHTEEN SIXTY-FIVE began with the armies of Grant and Lee still facing each other in Virginia across the massive front that had grown out of Grant's attempt to take Petersburg many months before. It was similar on the surface to 1864, but in reality everything was different. Lee's army was still in the field, but it was a dwindling army that had been punished by another year of unrelenting combat against superior forces with a never-ending supply of reinforcements and material. Atlanta was now gone, and Sherman was in Savannah, preparing for his final move on South Carolina, the state where it had all started four years before with the bombardment of Fort Sumter. If Lee's Army of Northern Virginia was hurting, the remnants of the Confederate Army of the Tennessee were also on the ropes in the face of Sherman's plans.

But the first significant military action of 1865 was in none of these places. Instead, it took place in North Carolina, where Union troops under Gen. Alfred H. Terry took Fort Fisher on January 15 and neutralized the city of Wilmington, the last place from which Confederate blockade runners had been able to function. As Sherman began to move from Georgia to South Carolina, the situation in many areas of the Confederacy were growing increasingly desperate, with shortages of food, medicine, and nearly all other kinds of supplies. Desertions from the various military units had increased to the point where the Confederacy considered, and Jefferson Davis approved, a plan to arm the slaves to fight on their side if they would, but this hopeless plan was never implemented.

In February, Jefferson Davis made overtures about a negotiated peace with the North, but his proposed plan involved Union recognition of the Confederacy's independence and never progressed. A few weeks later, on March 4, Lincoln had his second inauguration. At the end of March, Lee mounted an attack on Grant's forces near Petersburg and lost badly. A second attempt on April 1 had the same result. On April 2, Lee evacuated Richmond and headed west, hoping to link up with other forces. By April 7, Grant had Lee's remaining force surrounded and he sent the Confederate commander a now-famous battlefield letter. In his letter, Grant pointed out that Lee must now realize that his cause was hopeless, and he asked Lee to surrender to avoid further bloodshed. Lee agreed, and on April 9, surrendered the Army of Northern Virginia to Grant at Appomattox Courthouse, Virginia, the seat of Appomattox County, a little country crossroads twenty-five miles east of Lynchburg. Lee's soldiers were allowed to return to their homes and keep their horses for use in spring plowing; officers retained their personal arms. All other military equipment was surrendered. Other Confederate units, spread out throughout the South, surrendered at various locations during the following several weeks. Jefferson Davis, who had fled Richmond when Lee evacuated the city on April 2, was captured by Union forces in Georgia on May 10.

On April 14, just five days after Lee's surrender at Appomattox, President Lincoln was shot by John Wilkes Booth as he was watching a play, *Our American Cousin*, at Ford's Theater in Washington, D.C. He died the following morning. Eleven days later, Booth was shot and killed by a Union soldier in a burning barn in Virginia, where he had been cornered by a military search party. Of the nine other people involved in the assassination plot, four were hanged, four were imprisoned, and one was acquitted. No evidence that the Confederate military command or political leadership had any direct involvement with the assassination of Lincoln ever surfaced. Jefferson Davis, held for a time on suspicion of complicity in the plot against Lincoln, was eventually released. Like many others who played a central role in the Civil War, Davis returned to his home, lived quietly, and wrote his memoirs. On December 18, 1865, the Thirteenth Amendment to the Constitution, abolishing slavery, was ratified.

165

**165.** Marching through the swamps; a scene from Sherman's Southern campaign. Sherman's strategy on the way to Atlanta was fundamentally different from the strategy that had been uppermost in the Union command's thinking when the war began in 1861. This was a different kind of warfare; Sherman wasn't attacking an enemy army, he was attacking a state. His strategy was to decimate the state's entire means of support for the armies opposing him, and to destroy morale by devastating the countryside, farms, factories, railroads, and whatever else was in his path.

166

**166.** Sherman's army entering Columbia, South Carolina, in February 1865. Sherman left Atlanta in November 1864, leaving the city burning. He first turned it into a military base for his future operations and then destroyed it. He took Savannah just before Christmas and in February 1865, turned his 60,000-man army north to South Carolina. It was very clear at the time that this was an effort to punish the state where it had all begun, a move to devastate South Carolina for Fort Sumter and everything that had happened since. Charleston fell to the U.S. Navy on February 17; Sherman's attention was on the state capital at Columbia, which he occupied and burned.

167

**167.** March 1865, foragers start out. Sherman's army lived off the land with a vengeance, taking what they needed and sometimes just what they wanted.

**168.** March 1865, foragers return to camp. The two central figures on horseback seem to have found some objects worth taking. The behavior of Sherman's army in Georgia was probably not as bad as sometimes portrayed for propaganda purposes, but it was bad enough. Part of the strategy was to devastate the country psychologically, and controls were limited. It was a far cry from the officers and gentlemen of an earlier era.

168

169

170

171

**169.** Action at James Island, South Carolina, in February 1865, part of the attack on Charleston and the surrounding country. Sherman left the coastal operations such as this one to the Navy; he was busy contending with his former nemesis, Joseph E. Johnston, now back in command of the Confederate Army of the Tennessee.

**170.** An episode from Sherman's march into South Carolina in the last days of the war, the battle near Kinston on March 8, 1865.

**171.** The Battle of Bentonville, North Carolina, on March 21,

1865. Johnston had very little to lose and tried a final throw of the dice at Bentonville, firing everything he had at Sherman's superior army. It was a gamble he lost. A few weeks after Bentonville, Lee surrendered the Army of Northern Virginia to Grant, and Johnston was alone. With no hope left, the end came for the Army of the Tennessee on April 26 when Johnston surrendered to Sherman at Durham, North Carolina. Other scattered Confederate units followed suit in the following weeks. The war was really over when the last Confederate commander in the field, Gen. Kirby Smith, surrendered at New Orleans on May 26.

172

173

174

**172.** March 1865, Negro Quarters, Army of the James, part of the massive force arrayed against the remnants of Lee's Army of Northern Virginia which, in the final weeks of the war, had shrunk to about one-quarter the size of the force that Grant had at his command. The events of the last weeks of the war seem to proceed with a sense of inevitability. In early March 1865, Sheridan captured what was left of Early's command at Waynesboro and headed east to join Grant, who was determined not to allow Lee to escape Petersburg. On March 25, Lee attacked the Union army at Fort Stedman, hoping either to break Grant's hold on Petersburg or to divert enough of Grant's forces so that the rest of Lee's army could withdraw. It was a gamble that cost Lee 4,500 casualties. On April 1, a Union victory at Five Forks, seventeen miles southwest of Petersburg, proved to be the break in the Confederate defense that Grant had been waiting for. With his position crumbling, Lee advised Jefferson Davis that Petersburg and Richmond could not be held and headed west with his troops. Richmond and Petersburg were immediately occupied. Lee's plan was to follow the line of the Richmond & Danville Railroad to try to link up with other units still in the field at Danville and to reach supplies

that he hoped would be there. None of this worked, and on April 5, Lee found Sheridan's cavalry in his path and diverted northwest toward Lynchburg. Within two more days, Lee realized he was trapped and surrendered to Grant at 2 P.M. on Palm Sunday, April 9, 1865, in the farmhouse of Wilmer McLean at Appomattox Courthouse, Virginia. Three days later, 28,231 soldiers of the Army of Northern Virginia gave up their weapons and battle flags.

**173.** Ruins of Richmond, Main Street, April 1865. Jefferson Davis left Richmond on April 2, at the same time that Lee evacuated his army. The ruins in this illustration show the combined result of several devastating fires, some of which were started by Confederate soldiers who burned military supplies before evacuating Richmond, and others started by looters after the army was gone.

**174.** President Lincoln riding through Richmond, Virginia, April 4, 1865, amid the enthusiastic cheers of the inhabitants. It has always been said that the president was warmly greeted by the black population of Richmond, while others remained in their homes.

175

176

177

**175.** Grand Review at Washington, Sherman's veterans marching through Pennsylvania Avenue with the Capitol in the background, May 1865.

**176.** An illustration published at the end of the war of the burial grounds at Andersonville prison, the notorious prison camp in southwest central Georgia, where over 40,000 Union prisoners were held in 1864 and 1865 and where over 12,000 of them were buried. Neither side did a humane job of taking care of the huge number of military prisoners that escalated when the Union ended the agreement to exchange prisoners in the summer of 1863. Conditions at Andersonville were similar to conditions at other prison camps, North and South—polluted water; no sanitation; little or poor food, medical care, and shelter from the elements; and no protection against overcrowding, disease, and violence.

The scale of Andersonville made it especially shocking—it was a 26-acre camp where thousands died. After the war the Confederate commander of Andersonville, Captain Henry Wirz, was tried by a military commission and hanged in the yard of Washington's Old Capitol Prison on November 10, 1865.

**177.** Lincoln at home, April 1865, with his son Tad, in an illustration published in *Harper's* after the assassination. Lincoln had first arrived to take office in Washington by train, unannounced and unpublicized, in March 1861, as threats were rampant in the weeks leading up to start of the war and the police feared for his safety. When his body left Washington by train for its final journey to Springfield, Illinois, in April 1865, it was reported that seven million people turned out along the way to watch it go by.

# INDEX

*References are to page numbers, **not** figure numbers.*